Loneliness

The Anatomy of Loneliness by Thomas Wolfe

My life, more than that of anyone I know, has been spent in solitude and wandering. Why this is true, or how it happened, I cannot say; yet it is so. From my fifteenth year—save for a single interval—I have lived about as solitary a life as a modern man can have. I mean by this that the number of hours, days, months, and years that I have spent alone has been immense and extraordinary. I propose, therefore, to describe the experience of human loneliness exactly as I have known it.

The reason that impels me to do this is not that I think my knowledge of loneliness different in kind from that of other men. Quite the contrary. The whole conviction of my life now rests upon the belief that loneliness, far from being a rare and curious phenomenon, peculiar to myself and to a few other solitary men, is the central and inevitable fact of human existence. When we examine the moments, acts, and statements of all kinds of people—not only the grief and ecstasy of the greatest poets, but also the huge unhappiness of the average soul, as evidenced by the innumerable strident words of abuse, hatred, contempt, mistrust, and scorn that forever grate upon our ears as the manswarm passes us in the streets—we find, I think, that they are all suffering from the same thing. The final cause of their complaint is loneliness.

But if my experience of loneliness has not been different in kind from that of other men, I suspect it has been sharper in intensity. This gives me the best authority in the world to write of this, our general complaint, for I believe I know more about it than anyone of my generation. In saying this, I am merely stating a fact as I see it, though I realize that it may sound like arrogance or vanity. But before anyone jumps to that conclusion, let him consider how strange it would be to meet with arrogance in one who has lived alone as much as I. The surest cure for vanity is loneliness. For, more than other men, we who dwell in the heart of solitude are always the victims of self-doubt. Forever and forever in our loneliness, shameful feelings of inferiority will rise up suddenly to overwhelm us in a poisonous flood of horror, disbelief, and desolation, to sicken and corrupt our health and confidence, to spread pollution at the very root of strong, exultant joy. And the eternal paradox of it is that if a man is to know the triumphant labor of creation, he must for long periods resign himself to loneliness, and suffer loneliness to rob him of the health, the confidence, the belief and joy which are essential to creative work.

To live alone as I have lived, a man should have the confidence of God, the tranquil faith of a monastic saint, the stern impregnability of Gibraltar. Lacking these, there are times when anything, everything, all or nothing, the most trivial incidents, the most casual words, can in an instant strip me of my armor, palsy my hand, constrict my heart with frozen horror, and fill my bowels with the gray substance of shuddering impotence. Sometimes it is nothing but a shadow passing on the sun; sometimes nothing but the torrid milky light of August, or the naked, sprawling ugliness and squalid decencies of streets in Brooklyn fading in the weary vistas of that milky light and evoking the intolerable misery of countless drab and nameless lives. Sometimes it is just the barren horror of raw concrete, or the heat blazing on a million beetles of machinery darting through the torrid streets, or the cindered weariness of parking spaces, or the slamming smash and racket of the El, or the driven manswarm of the earth, thrusting on forever in exacerbated fury, going nowhere in a hurry.

Again, it may be just a phrase, a look, a gesture. It may be the cold, disdainful inclination of the head with which a precious, kept, exquisite princeling of Park Avenue acknowledges an introduction, as if to say: "You are nothing." Or it may be a sneering reference and dismissal by a critic in a high-class weekly magazine. Or a letter from a woman saying I am lost and ruined, my talent vanished, all my efforts false and worthless—since I have forsaken the truth, vision, and reality which are so beautifully her own.

And sometimes it is less than these—nothing I can touch or see or hear or definitely remember. It may be so vague as to be a kind of hideous weather of the soul, subtly compounded of all the hunger, fury, and impossible desire my life has ever known. Or, again, it may be a half-forgotten memory of the cold wintry red of waning Sunday afternoons in Cambridge, and of a pallid, sensitive, aesthetic face that held me once in earnest discourse on such a Sunday afternoon in Cambridge, telling me that all my youthful hopes were pitiful delusions and that all my life would come to naught, and the red and waning light of March was reflected on the pallid face with a desolate impotence that instantly quenched all the young ardors of my blood.

Beneath the evocations of these lights and weathers, and the cold, disdainful words of precious, sneering, and contemptuous people, all of the joy and singing of the day goes out like an extinguished candle, hope seems lost to me forever, and every truth that I have ever found and known seems false. At such a time the lonely man will feel that all the evidence of his own senses has betrayed him, and that nothing really lives and moves on earth but creatures of the death-in-life—those of the cold, constricted heart and the sterile loins, who exist forever in the red waning light of March and Sunday afternoon.

All this hideous doubt, despair, and dark confusion of the soul a lonely man must know, for he is united to no image save that which he creates himself, he is bolstered by no other knowledge save that which he can gather for himself with the vision of his own eyes and brain. He is sustained and cheered and aided by no party, he is given comfort by no creed, he has no faith in him except his own. And often that faith deserts him, leaving him shaken and filled with impotence. And then it seems to him that his life has come to nothing, that he is ruined, lost, and broken past redemption, and that morning—bright, shining morning, with its promise of new beginnings—will never come upon the earth again as it did once.

He knows that dark time is flowing by him like a river. The huge, dark wall of loneliness is around him now. It encloses and presses in upon him, and he cannot escape. And the cancerous plant of memory is feeding at his entrails, recalling hundreds of forgotten faces and ten thousand vanished days, until all life seems as strange and insubstantial as a dream. Time flows by him like a river, and he waits in his little room like a creature held captive by an evil spell. And he will hear, far off, the murmurous drone of the great earth, and feel that he has been forgotten, that his powers are wasting from him while the river flows, and that all his life has come to nothing. He feels that his strength is gone, his power withered, while he sits there drugged and fettered in the prison of his loneliness.

Then suddenly, one day, for no apparent reason, his faith and his belief in life will come back to him in a tidal flood. It will rise up in him with a jubilant and invincible power, bursting a window in the world's great wall and restoring everything to shapes of deathless brightness. Made miraculously whole and secure in himself, he will plunge once more into the triumphant labor of creation. All his old strength is his again: he knows what he knows, he is what he is, he has found what he has found. And he will say the truth that is in him, speak it even though the whole world deny it, affirm it though a million men cry out that it is false.

"The Anatomy of Loneliness," by Thomas Wolfe, appeared in *The American Mercury*, October 1941, and, as "God's Lonely Man," in *The Hills Beyond*, by Thomas Wolfe, Copyright, 1941 by Maxwell Perkins, as Executor; reprinted by permission of Harper & Row, Publishers, Inc.

Introduction

While I was preparing this book I met two or three hundred people, some of whom I have got to know very well indeed. I met them in many ways—through friends, social workers, voluntary organisations, letters to newspapers, but most of all by simply being around in pubs, parks, launderettes and shops. None of the people in the text of this book is institutionalised. They are all more or less fending for themselves in society, and much of their suffering is silent and unnoticed. It is in no way a cross-section of the population, nor is it intended to be a catalogue of all the known scourges of mankind. Quite a large section of the book deals with loneliness in 'normal' and unexceptional circumstances: in marriage and in relationships between parents and children.

Many people's loneliness tends to be made worse by our society. It may be impossible to prevent old age, bereavement or the decay of relationships but their effect on the individual may be mitigated by societies other than ours. A consumer-orientated, hedonistic society encourages expectations which cannot be fulfilled and results in frustration for the individual who finds that acquisitions do not necessarily lend a new dimension to personality.

Loneliness is a subject surrounded by prohibitions and embarrassments. Those affected by it are caught up in a spiral of self-reinforcing isolation. Many who suffer from it feel that it is the result of personal un-worthiness. It is something they are ashamed of. In order to be able to talk about it, they must have circumstances, or better still, individuals to blame.

Some of the circumstances in which people are compelled to live out their lives are desperate. But the accounts they give of themselves in these interviews often show an extraordinary determination to survive in spite of overwhelming handicaps and disadvantages. The impression which emerges is not at all negative and pessimistic. I have concealed the identities by altering details, but I have tried to get across the feeling of the life of each individual as it was conveyed to me. I did not use a tape recorder, except in one or two instances.

Usually I preferred to transcribe conversations from memory, even though this meant there would be some omissions of recall. I have simply tried to recreate something of each encounter with a lonely person. It has sometimes been a delicate and painful experience, and I can only hope I have not added to the burden of isolation by any misrepresentation or want of feeling.

Mr Reid

Mr. Reid is a retired window-cleaner of eighty-eight living off his pension and savings. His wife died last year and he has one son in Australia, one in Birmingham and a daughter in the same town. He owns the neat, carefully-maintained terrace house where he has lived for the past fifty-eight years.

The interior of his house is austere and old-fashioned: little has been added to the furniture since the nineteen thirties, apart from a bed in the front room. The bed has not been made for some time, and the sheets form a crumpled canopy over a depression in the mattress where Mr Reid habitually lies. In the living room there is a dresser in black wood with willow-pattern plates and dishes ranged along the shelves. There is a rag rug on the floor and a battered rocking chair under the window.

It is the morning before Christmas, the first Christmas for fifty-three years that he has been without his wife. Mr Reid is reading through a cookery book of the nineteen twenties trying to find out how to cook a piece of frozen chicken. I suggest to him that such an old book is unlikely to be helpful about frozen foods.

I like it boiled. It says here 'boiled with white sauce', I don't want no white sauce or any other coloured sauce. My son's coming to fetch me Christmas Day, so I shall have my Christmas dinner with them. They've got a big house, paid three thousand for it; it's worth six now. Big windows — it's like sitting in a shop window all day. I had a fall down their stairs. I like being in my own little home.

I left school when I was eleven. I went making coffins. Then the next year I left home. My pal was going bill-posting in Bedford and I wanted to go with him. My mother she didn't want me to go, but my Dad said 'Let him go, it'll make a man of him.' Ah! Eleven! When we were kids we used to go out in the fields and gather all the herbs, medicines and poultices; didn't need doctors. You couldn't do it now; they've killed everything. I used to get stinking nanny — stinking nanny it was called,— you rubbed it over your leg for a bruise, and in twenty-four hours it'd be gone. My grandma, she used to send me out with a pair of scissors and a big sack and make me gather all the stinging nettles I could find. She'd dry them and chop them up — well they broke up by themselves — and then she'd make a drink like tea. She had a drink of it every morning and she never had rheumatism or cramps in all her life. And she lived to be over ninety. Of course there's a lot of complaints about today there never used to be. Life was easier. There was bags of good meat about, more meat than you could eat. And cheap! You could get a damn good meal for twopence. All you needed was a ha'p'orth of pot-herbs and a penn'orth of shin. We all kept a pig. Oh it was a glorious time, pig-killing time. They'd render the lard down, make pig's pudding, chitterlings. I used to pride myself I could turn a pig's belly in two minutes.

There was never all the carry-on there is today. All this hooliganism, the trade unions, there was nothing of that. And we were better for it. My mother was in service with the Rothschilds. Put her the side of Queen Victoria, you wouldn't have been able to tell them apart. The Rothschilds went to America, and my mother should've gone with them by rights, but she was carrying me and she was frightened to go across the water.

I can tell the future you know. I get a feeling something's going to happen, and it does. I don't always tell people about it, it upsets them. I get a feeling across my forehead if I meet somebody who's going to have an accident. The world's going to end you know. In 1991. You'll see. The reason is nine and one that makes ten, you can't go any higher than ten. One and nine and nine and one. That's ten twice over, that's as far as it can go. Time. And the end of the world'll come through a terrific storm. Same as it did last time. It'll last for forty days and forty nights, and the world'll end through fire. It'll burn all the grass up, the trees, everything. Everything in its path'll be destroyed. Thunder and lightning and fire. Look at all the electricity there is. Look at these wireless aerials. Once the lightning strikes that aerial, it's going to set fire to the house because lightning can go through any wall. It'll come through anything. You can have the curtains drawn and lightning will come through the curtains, set anything afire. The metal draws it — a watch chain, money in your pocket, anything made of metal. The petrol in the cars, everything standing in the street, they'll be alight in no time. Well you'd be burnt to death if these streets were all alight, you wouldn't be able to run anywhere. Where could you run?

I shan't be here to see it. I shall be with mother... She was a good old gal. We had fifty-three years together. Long time, but it's never just long enough is it?

[*He shows me a photograph of her taken at their Golden Wedding party; posed and smiling. The whole room spoke of her absence, of the incipient neglect of a household from which the woman has disappeared. Her death was an amputation he still feels. His conversation is full of what she would have said if she had been here.*] She'd go mad if she knew I was eating frozen chicken. There can't be the goodness in it. It's a funny thing, she wanted me to give up smoking for years; and when she died I stopped. Just like that. If she can see me I wonder what she's thinking. I'll tell you what I would like, though — a bottle of beer. And you can give me a hand with this coupon before you go. What's forty-two rows at a sixteenth of a penny a go?

It is not simply that Mr Reid has been mutilated of a lifetime's companionship. He represents a cultural tradition of which he is one of the last survivors. All his fellows have disappeared, and he is left standing on his doorstep repeating to passers-by an ancient and obsolete wisdom which his hearers mistake for senility.

13

Delia
Graham

Delia is thirty years old and a spastic. She has little use in her legs and arms, and her speech is so indistinct that only those who know her well really understand her. She communicates very effectively by typing with her nose. She is an intelligent and attractive person and has all the aids that the Social Services can provide, including a self-propelling chair and ingenious electronic devices that open the door, answer the telephone, etcetera. She has done A-level French and English; she writes, and has had some poetry published in an international anthology. She paints and goes to evening classes on literature and painting. She is married to a clerical worker, and lives on a council estate, in a ground-floor flat, in Leeds.

Her talents and abilities are seriously under-used by the society she lives in and she is forced to regret her education and insight, and to wish often she could be the non-sentient creature which people take her for. The desperation of her immobility and dependence upon others, and at the same time her fierce and questioning intelligence, leads to a kind of frustration that it is difficult for others to perceive, let alone comprehend. She sometimes travels to Surrey, where she has friends. She goes by train, and carries notes of where she wants to get to, which she hands to porters, taxi-drivers, policemen, and which begin 'I am afraid I have no speech, but I assure you I'm not a moron or a nut-case, but I want to get to Camberley.' She delivers these requests, and then watches the recipient put them in his pocket, panic, make excuses, fetch help, when her needs for help are really very modest and easy to fulfil.

The first time I saw Delia she was in a state of despair. She said that she has always been a fighter, but she is increasingly subject to feelings of hopelessness, especially in those areas where it is widely and naively believed that the battles have already been won—among the physically handicapped. The devolution of responsibility for the disabled upon the Social Services means that other people don't need to bother. Together with all the gadgetry that technology can devise, beneficently harnessed to human need, Delia has been burdened with society's conviction that she should consider herself lucky and ask for nothing more than to exist. As conditions for the disabled—or the poor, or the mentally ill— improve, we tend to compare them with the conditions from which they have advanced, and not with conditions as they should be. As improvements occur—and Delia is the first to admit that her position is far better than that of the institutionalised wreckage she would have been in previous generations—great new gulfs open up; new areas of unfulfilled need come to light. The social battles have scarcely begun: to rattle our unwanted small change in the tin marked Spastics doesn't discharge our obligations to Delia. She is always there, sensitive, intelligent, monitoring our every recoil and evasion.

Having been at boarding-school from the age of six, and then at a college for disabled young people for several years, I hadn't really experienced true loneliness until I got married and found myself in the so-called community. I had always been surrounded by people, sometimes too many, but I think now that my own company is a good deal worse.

My parents never mollycoddled me, and anyway, being away from home for most of the time I had to learn to stand on my own feet pretty fast, as opposed to being crushed and institutionalised. My college years were the real making of me, I think. They were tough years, but having to stick up for your rights and having to make decisions for myself, made me what I am — and I think I can claim to be a fighter. My social life was rich. As our college was fairly near the University of Essex, many of my friends were students there. Apart from study, there were parties, theatre and cinema trips, a folk and jazz club. But you can't remain a student all your life.

I got married, and that's when I first realised what a terrible monster loneliness was. There was suddenly no more popping up the corridor for a chat, no more heated discussions. No more people. OK, I had a husband, but I was alone all day. First of all we rented rooms — the kitchen being on the ground floor, while our other two rooms were up a steep flight of stairs. During the day I had to sit in the kitchen, which had no window. The house was owned by an Italian family who were very kind and used to pop in sometimes, but then there was the language problem to add to my communication difficulties. (My speech is bad and only those chosen few can understand me verbally — usually I speak via my typewriter.)

I thought I couldn't possibly feel more isolated, having left college and Colchester, where most of my friends were. Leeds seemed to epitomise the town of loneliness. I didn't know anyone. I used to read a lot and write letters from my kitchen prison, and hope this kind of existence wouldn't last too long. In an optimistic mood one day I wrote to the local paper asking them to publish a letter to the effect that I was new to the city, an extrovert, interested in art and poetry — lonely, cut off and longing to meet anyone who cared to call. Hopefully, I thought, that might help brighten my days, which were enormously long. But no such luck. The editor wrote back saying they couldn't print it because it might encourage cranks and other undesirables. I thought, well that's what I want, anything for a bit of excitement. If the editor had known the situations I'd been in and the experiences I'd had, he might have sat up with a jerk. It was just that my damn wheelchair symbolised helplessness — pooh. ROT.

I next tried to go to the Tech. to carry on with my painting, but here too, they didn't want to know. My wheelchair was again the excuse.

My life carried on in this way for about six months. Then we were offered a council flat — a light in my darkness, I thought. It was a ground floor flat — everything on one level, which meant I could move from room to room and actually look out of the windows. I could see people and lots of children. So — a home of our own. Everything looked super, and I was sure I'd be much happier.

I'd heard that council estates were very lonely places, but it didn't bother me much. I had never lived on one. I thought after the initial shock of having a disabled person in their street — and with a wheelchair too! — my neighbours would be overcome with curiosity, if nothing else, and would come to meet me. I saw them popping in and out of each other's houses, borrowing sugar maybe, drinking endless cups of coffee and gossiping away. But again I was wrong, and my optimism and faith in people took another bashing. After three and a half years I can honestly say I only knew the people next door, who have since moved.

Why? I think the answer is mainly FEAR. Fear, not only of my physical disability and communication problems, but also fear of becoming INVOLVED. Nasty. Who knows what I might ask them to do?... I daren't ask people to stop by sometimes because of this. Of course, it would be super if people called in to make a cup of coffee, but more than coffee I need company, conversation, stimulation, PEOPLE.

Then there is the other fear. Half the neighbourhood thinks, I'm sure, that I'm not quite all there, or maybe I may get violent (and leap out of my wheelchair and assault them), or maybe I might foam at the mouth and have a fit (not part of my disability, I must add). My speech doesn't help, but with my typewriter I can have as good a conversation as anyone. And if they would only come and see for themselves, they'd find I'm not deaf, dumb or daft.

On the other hand, the other half of the neighbourhood thinks I'm too highbrow, with all my GCEs etcetera, but again, if only they would come and see, they'd find I'm certainly not an intellectual snob. I long for people, and always find them interesting, and I at least always have something to say.

When I go out, people aren't hostile. They usually say hello, and even several streets away know my name, so my existence is not unknown. A great joke is when people walk past my window, they invariably look in and *wave*. Big deal. Let's give her a wave, they must think, and make her day. A nice gesture, granted, but God, gestures are gestures.

I don't want people coming in and offering help — just a little company. It's the dark evenings that get me down, and sometimes make me feel quite deadly. I can switch the light on with the aid of my Possum, and this acts as a sort of spotlight and passers-by wave even more, but if they'd only come in and draw my curtains! It really gets me down. But again, it must be fear. Another example of this is when I ring my external alarm bell, which isn't very often, as I've not experienced murder yet. When I have rung it, it has been because an electrical gadget hasn't been plugged in, or when I drop all my paper on the floor and can't type. But each time, it has always been TWO women coming in. And then, they're in and out like lightning. I know I'm biassed, but I'm sure I don't look that peculiar or terrifying — maybe my mirror is wonky.

Shylock's moving speech comes into my mind, where he is trying to get across the fact that although he is a Jew he is just as human as anyone else. In the same way, just because I have a physical disability, I *am* just as human as the next person — with a mind, feelings, emotions. I don't think the people around here can be under the illusion that spasticity is a catching disease, but it makes you wonder really.

One day, my telephone had to be fixed. The GPO men just happened to come at a time when my home help was here. It was a very complex affair, and they said they would come back the following day, but asked if anyone would be with me. I said (wishing my typewriter had a voice like Eartha Kitt) 'No, I'll be alone', adding 'But I won't eat you'. The ice broke, and the next day we had quite a fun time. They found me rather amusing and cheered me up too.

If only the neighbours would take the first step and come in and see. They know *I* can't get out by myself and make the first move. I thought my Possum equipment would interest them, as it is fun, and new to the city. I put notes in the nearby houses, explaining about my alarm bell, but even that didn't arouse their curiosity. Dead souls — and I'm so alive — that's another difference between us. Or should I say I'd like to be alive, and to live and to give, but before this can happen I have to fight the unnecessary battle of proving my normality — my being a part of the human race — which shouldn't have to be fought. I KNOW it needn't be fought, because when in the right company — as recently, when I stayed in a commune set up with university students — I was absolutely NO DIFFERENT from anyone else in the house. And when you know you're no different, it's so hard to accept the attitude of the public in general.

I know that loneliness enters most people's lives at some time, but obviously disabled people, those confined to a chair are more a prey to it. However, I know that if I had a happy (or successful) marriage, I should be able to put up with the loneliness of the long days. I should look forward to my husband coming home, to doing things together, to going out, to conversation, stimulation... But this is not the way it is. The evenings, when my husband is here at home, are just as lonely. Conversation is almost nil, and we have nothing in common. If I were less extrovert, less intelligent, and more of a stuffed marrow, things would be better. But I have been used to LIVING, not just existing. When I think of my life stretching out in a similar pattern to the past three years, I scream out inside in absolute desperation, Stagnation, stagnation, stagnation, the word goes round in my head. I don't want to waste my life in this way, but what is the escape route? I read, paint, write poetry and go to a couple of classes — yet it is difficult to paint without inspiration, to write poetry without some external stimulation, and although I read, it's not half as much as I used to — who is there to discuss things with?

Loneliness when you're alone is reasonable, something to be overcome, but loneliness when you're with someone is a great deal less tolerable.

Why did I get myself into this predicament, then? I mean, that of marriage. I had always been anti-marriage.

When I was twenty-two, and had had quite a few affairs, I was proposed to (not for the first time) by someone I'd known for several years, but not intimately. I refused, but he was persistent, and eventually he agreed to our living together for a year or whatever amount of time was necessary. Gullible as always, I believed him. I gave up my place at college and my plans for art school and came to Leeds. However, when I arrived, things were not as I thought. His religious beliefs (which I thought another fad he was going through — he had been through so many) got the better of him, and he insisted constantly on our marriage.

I agreed; and then found myself trapped. I couldn't return to college, nor go home, as my parents can't cope; so there I was with marriage staring me in the face. A stupid piece of paper was signed and all was well in the sight of God.

At first, I really made an effort, I tried to make something of our relationship, hoping all the while that my husband's religiosity would die down and eventually fade out. But this didn't happen — in fact, he has become even more fervent and any conversation we may have must always come back to this subject. I'm not intolerant, but I can't share his views at all.

I don't think I've told anyone before, but when I agreed to live with my now husband (and I confess my arrogance and naive outlook), I had in mind doing a Ronnie stunt as in Wesker's play *Roots*. I had had the same sort of making thrust on me by a boy-friend at college. But it didn't take me long to find out how stupid I had been to have such notions. I soon found we had very little in common; and the religious conflict (I am an atheist) was no help. In the end I stopped trying.

Life went on in the same monotonous way, and I hated Leeds more and more, and the council estate too. I was in exile... Indefinitely. As well as my matrimonial difficulties, I found the natives unfriendly — not in any hostile way, just negatively so.

I enrolled in the Open University, aiming at corres-
pondence teaching, but gave it up after a year, finding
it difficult and discouraging to study by myself. They
even refused to have me on the Summer School,
which I was looking forward to, not only as an aca-
demic boost, but a social break too.

It was during that year that, seeing no other
possible solution, I attempted suicide by taking an
overdose. It was NOT meant to be a gesture, I could
see no other practical way out of my predicament. I
am not what is termed a neurotic character. It certainly wasn't a gesture when I think what a struggle it
was — it took me an hour and a half to open the
damn bottle. So time ran out. I was found too soon. I
went to hospital, where I saw a psychiatrist, who said
the solution to my matrimonial problem was to have
a child... something which I still can't get over.
LUDICROUS.

Out of hospital — home — and back to the same
life. Couldn't people see what a hell my marriage
was? No. It took me another year to screw up enough
courage to find myself a solicitor in order to get a
divorce. However, it hasn't got me very far — after
eight months. The whole thing is tragi-comic. I have
to see a psychiatrist, as they are considered experts
and an expert's opinion will strengthen my case.
Really, I'm NOT neurotic. Had I had a couple of
breakdowns, it would no doubt help. I saw one head-
shrinker, but his report was considered 'too vague' by
the barrister, so I was put under another, who must
be either extremely popular or overworked, as my
appointment can't be for three months.

I know I'm quite sane and won't go off the rails,
but I have to be careful as to who I tell, because
people tend to feel sorry for me, and thus the relationship becomes bent and invariably falls through.

*Implicit in the declared need for psychiatric re-
ports before divorce can be considered, is the
assumption that she must be mad to throw away her
security like that, when she has so many handicaps.
Delia is denied the right to criticise her marriage,*

because, it is felt, she should consider herself lucky.

She is not a sad or depressed person. Her room was full of the objects with which she tries to lead a meaningful life—volumes of poetry, mainly twentieth century, the works of Camus, William Golding, Sartre, her paintings, a vase of roses, cacti and plants grown from melon-seeds, a large tabby cat and a gerbil in a cage. It was always mornings when I saw her. Outside, the estate was almost deserted; one or two under-fives playing, but most of the doors shut, the milk bottles on the doorstep; an industrial barrack-block, a dormitory for workers, in which Delia is a painful and self-conscious anomaly.

Mr Blandford

Mr Blandford is a fifty-nine year old widower living off Social Security in a privately-rented flat in South London. I walked down a long row of Edwardian villas looking at the bay windows with foliate carving, cracked tessellated courtyards, privet hedges and fragments of ironwork railings. Many of the houses have been turned into flats, not for multi-occupation, but into two apartments, with only the vestibule shared, a ghostly neutral space of dusty cornices and thistle-carvings speaking of ceremonial arrivals and departures that the present occupants know nothing of.

Mr Blandford lives in the upstairs flat. The stairs spiral upwards to a spacious landing, dark and windowless, where the breath condenses and there is a faint smell of mildew—perhaps from behind the corrugating wallpaper in pale Regency stripes. The living room is what was originally the master bedroom of the house. It is neat and orderly: there are many pictures and ornaments but they do not manage to abolish the oppressive sense of space. The objects in the room date chiefly from the 'fifties — maroon moquette chairs with wooden arms and timidly abstract designs, upright dining chairs, a china cabinet. A china model of two Mabel Lucie Attwell lovers on a rustic bench stands on top of the gas-fire.

Mr Blandford lives alone and sees virtually no one. He gets a disability pension for his emphysema, and receives just under £10 a week. When I visited it was 28 December. He had spoken to no one since 23 December, and then it had been to the counter-clerk at the Post Office where he collects his pension. For Christmas dinner he had eaten a tin of Irish stew.

Mr Blandford is thin, and possibly under-nourished: a nervous, methodical man, who likes everything in its place. He was a driver on London Transport underground for most of his working life, but then became a rat-catcher for a South London borough until he was forced to retire after a long

illness. His wife died eleven years ago. He has tried,
unsuccessfully to find someone to share the flat. He
showed me the whole flat, kitchen, bathroom and the
one bedroom, in which there was a huge bed covered
with a pink candlewick bedspread. Pointing to the
bed, he said:

That's why I can't find anybody to share, that's the
reason. They see the bed and they think I just want
somebody for sex. I went to the borough Social Services. I said I'd got plenty of room. They sent somebody down to look at the flat and I never heard
another word from them. I went to the drug place
down Camberwell — same thing. They came to look
at it and said wouldn't it be better if I had two single
beds? How can I afford to buy single beds on £10 a
week?
   What I'd really like is a young woman, an unmarried mother with a child, somebody who'd be
grateful, be thankful to have somewhere to lay her
head. If sex came along I wouldn't mind, but if she
didn't want it, I'd just turn my back and go to sleep, I
wouldn't bother. But it really staggers me. They're
always saying there's an acute shortage of accommodation, and then when I offer my place, it seems they
don't want to know... Anyway, just because I've got a
double bed doesn't mean anything. I might be a
homosexual for all they know. I've been in the army,
I know what goes on, I might be a shit-tickler for all
they know. In the barracks where I was, anyone of
half a dozen blokes would've got into bed with me if
I'd wanted it. So that's no argument. I did have a girl
living here for a little while, she'd got a kiddie. I
didn't mind that, only she wanted to be out all
the while. She'd been living with a bloke who'd been
knocking her around, I thought well, she'll be glad of
somewhere to live and somebody to treat her decent.
But she was off in no time. She didn't want to know.
It makes you feel very bitter. I've tried putting cards
in all the shop windows. Nothing... I don't get any
sex life — masturbation and the occasional

prostitute — I'm not expected to spend the rest of my life like this am I?

I was happy with my wife. Well, we had our ups and downs. She died of pneumonia; they took her into hospital at one o'clock in the morning. By three o'clock she was dead. I just don't remember how I got back here from the hospital that night; it's a blank in my memory.

I've got three children, all boys. None of them want to know. Two of them live near here, the other one lives in Kent. They've all got good jobs, but I never see them. Never any help. They wouldn't ask me over to spend Christmas, any of them. I did call in on the one down New Cross. He married a woman who'd already got two kids, and he's knocked three more out of her already. I told him I'd had nothing from Ken — that's the oldest boy, and he said 'Well I've got this expense, I've got that expense, just had the car done, central heating put in, holidays, the kids' shoes'. Anyway he goes and tells Ken what I told him, and the next thing I know, this is what I get from Ken [*he fetches out a letter, perhaps three months old*]. 'Dad, why do you keep stirring the shit. If you want to get any money, you're going the right way to get it aren't you. You might get some in a month or two (I don't promise) but only if you keep your nose out.'

I've had nothing from him. I got a quid from the other boy at Christmas. He's not too bad. The bloke who lives in the flat downstairs is better to me than my kids are.

I get this magazine, *In Depth*. I suppose Longford and his pals'd call it pornographic. They make me mad, when they come on TV, talking about pornography and permissiveness, I know I haven't seen much sign of it. They've got no right to interfere in people's lives like that. It's hard enough as it is, without them adding to it. Do you think this is pornography? [*He shows me a picture of a wind swept blonde on a piebald stallion in a woodland glade.*] I think it's beautiful. Thats what I'd like, somebody like that.

I need somebody to depend on me. there must be lots of people, young people, who get into trouble and need help. I wrote a letter to this magazine, explaining how things were. I got a nice letter back, so I wrote again. Next thing I get is a form offering me a list of addresses if I pay £3.50. Everybody wants money, that's all they're after.

I don't get any help. How am I supposed to pay the TV licence, out of ten pounds a week? I pay a quid a week off my gas-bill, it's never clear. If I had somebody to stay with me, I wouldn't charge her, just for food that's all. You can live much cheaper if there's two of you. I wouldn't mind who she was: I'm not prejudiced on colour or anything like that. I want somebody to look after. I'm not bothered about sex. But I don't want to live like this, do I?

Miss Houghton

Miss Houghton, who is sixty, lives off her savings. She used to be a boot and shoe operative but was made redundant. She has no family and for the last fifteen years has lived in a nineteen-twenties suburban villa with a low front wall and small garden paved with wooden tubs of hydrangeas. There is a chiming doorbell and stained glass in the front door. Inside, the house is cool, neat and spinsterish. A bowl of sweet peas, bright as butterflies, in the centre of a black wood gate-leg table; floral designs on carpet, curtains and chair-covers; much crochet work like ornamental cobwebs on all surfaces—table, sideboard, on the headrests of chairs. A tea-tray: ginger nuts, and more of the ubiquitous roses on the teacups.

Miss Houghton is small, with thinning white hair; she wears a navy blue and white dress, with a cameo brooch at the throat. She wears a navy blue straw hat, even indoors, perhaps to hide the pink patches of scalp which show through her falling hair.

I'm one of those people who aren't quite what they seem to be. I'm busy, active, I have friends, I help my neighbours, but I'm quite empty inside. I'm really a shell, there's no feeling left.

I'm a withered woman, you see. I mean it, quite literally. I'm wasted. I ought to have been married, I should have borne children. It's what I wanted above anything else. And I knew all the time that my life was passing, that I wasn't fulfilling myself. But I didn't really know why, and at that time I certainly couldn't have done anything about it. I've lived with hatred you see. Hatred and duty. That's why I say I'm not what I appear to be. I've got this terrible bitterness. Hatred and duty.

Sometimes human beings have too much power over each other. No human being should control the life of another as my mother controlled me. She tied me to her. I couldn't have left her any more than if we were chained together. I know it sounds melo-dramatic, I think perhaps it is. Ever since I was a young girl my mother was always ill. I always felt insecure, even as a child, because of my mother's health. She was always talking to me about being taken, and if I weren't a good girl God would take her away from me. At the time I only hated God for it... She was deserted by my father. He didn't come home from the war. She used to pretend that he was killed. When I was about twelve, I went to look for his name on the War Memorial in the centre of town, I don't know if you've seen it there. There are all the names of the heroes, columns and columns of them, all in gold. And of course his name wasn't there. I asked her why, and she said there wasn't room for all the names... I discovered afterwards that he was living only a few miles away with a French woman.

I suppose my mother felt unhappy and bitter herself, I was an only child. So she made sure that I didn't desert her. She worked, oh she worked so hard. We rented a small house, and she did dressmaking, mending, even making shoes at home. She had a last, and I think she made shoes — she certainly mended all mine and her own. But she ruled my life. I was made to feel that anybody I spoke to almost was an act of treachery to her in some way. I wasn't allowed friends. Nobody ever came inside our house. An aunt came to see us once a week. My grandmother, a woman I later knew to be my father's mother came occasionally, but never a friend of my own. I went to other girls' houses sometimes, and was amazed to find that they actually welcomed me. I came to imagine that there was something terribly wrong with our house, that no one ever came inside it. I knew we were poor, and I became ashamed of that, and told the most awful lies at school about my father and his wealth. I used to tell everybody he was a doctor.

If I went to tea with a girl-friend, my mother was angry for days afterwards. She'd say 'I don't want you to get too thick with them' and I'd say 'Oh, why?' And she'd say 'Never you mind', and it sounded so sinister, I thought she must surely know things about them I didn't. And I'd stop going. My mother possessed my mind. She made all the decisions for me. She preyed on a child's feeling of insecurity, instead of decreasing that feeling by reassuring and encouraging me. It was wicked, what she did to me. I tell myself now that it was because she was afraid of being alone in the world.

When I was terribly young, she made me promise not to let her go in the workhouse — before I even knew what the workhouse was. She got me up one Sunday morning and made me swear on the Bible not to let her finish up in the workhouse. I promised her I wouldn't, and then she'd comfort me and kiss me... But the really surprising thing is that I must have been nearly thirty before I realised what she was doing to me. You must remember that at that time, there wasn't the understanding; nobody knew about psychology and all that sort of thing. It was very easy to be crushed in a way that no young people would put up with today. In a way she shielded me from the world so well that no other influences came anywhere near me; and when they did she always had her illnesses to fall back on. I don't know if they were real or not; perhaps they were hysterical, she induced them herself. They were always vague. But she'd lie in bed for a few weeks, and Aunt Cis would come round and I had to tiptoe through the house so as not to disturb her.

I left school at fourteen and went to work in a factory. It was a brush factory. I was taken away from school the day after my fourteenth birthday — which should never have happened — and taken to work by my mother. Only the education authorities insisted at that time that you had to carry on to the end of the term after your fourteenth birthday, so after three days at work I was taken back to school. I thought they were going to let me stay on, and of course it was just what I wanted. But three weeks later I left school again, for good this time. I hated the factory. I read. I used to escape into books. I had nobody I could share things with. I read Dickens and Jane Austen and H. G. Wells and Bernard Shaw, but I was always aware that my interests were unusual, to say the least. In fact I was ashamed of it, and my workmates called me snobbish and stand-offish, which I resented, because I was neither of those things. That always distressed me. But I used to do things for them, help them to write letters, or speak to the boss for them, and in the end I was accepted. A bit eccentric....

My reading broadened me a great deal, but somehow I never applied any of the things I read to my own life. I just accepted that my mother was always there, and she required my constant attention. She taunted me with ingratitude — she used to refer to a mysterious life of happiness she might have had but for me. Of course it was untrue. She never had any men friends or anything like that.

Nor did I. At least not until I was twenty-eight, and that didn't last long. He was a man of thirty-eight, and his wife was mentally ill. She was in the asylum. He had two children, and although he worked in the same factory he was rather more gentle and refined than most of the men there. There was a sympathy between us. I don't mean refined in a snobbish way — it was just that we could exchange books. He gave me Robert Blatchford to read, and it was through him I heard of Alexandre Dumas. Isn't that silly reading books of adventure at nearly thirty. But I was enthralled.

We met sometimes for an hour in the evening, in the park. I shall never forget that summer. 1930. It was so still and calm, can you imagine, the trees and the evening sunshine. We never had any kind of physical relationship. He didn't even kiss me. It was the first experience of my life that wasn't dictated to me by my mother. It's the most precious memory I have. Anyway, this is a rather small town, and somebody must have seen us together and reported it to Aunt Cis, who immediately told mother. She didn't confront me with it, although if she had done so I would probably have stopped seeing him, because I felt guilty because of his wife. But she didn't. She became ill instead. She discovered that she had a weak heart, and she told me that if she had any shock, if she learned anything unpleasant about me, the shock would kill her. How I didn't see through it! I believed it. And I told Sydney that I should not see him again. She played upon my guilt. He left the factory soon afterwards, and I heard that he had abandoned his children.

After that, I began to reflect on what had happened, and I began to realise at that late age that I had been a victim of my mother's dependency on me. After that, it got so that I could anticipate her cunning. But I never succeeded in breaking away from her. I really was rather a timid creature. In one sense she'd already won her battle by the time I came to understand. I was always slightly afraid of people, of meeting people, getting involved. I did go out more, though. I went to evening classes, and I met people who could talk about literature and theatre. I got interested in archaeology, and even went on two or three summer holidays, working on sites in East Anglia and Southern England. Each time she tried to punish me by being ill. But I still went. You can't imagine what a triumph that seemed for my independence. I never made another relationship with a man.

I seemed to resign myself to very small satisfactions. I used to go out to literature class, and if I had a good book from the library I would hurry home from the factory as eagerly as though I were going to meet a lover. And I'd get mother's tea, and sit down, perhaps with only a boiled egg or bread and jam, and I'd put the book on the table, and really lose myself. It used to irritate her. She'd say 'Kitty, it's bad manners to put books on the tea-table', and she'd want me to talk to her. But I had nothing but coldness for her then. I really felt nothing at all. Of course, nobody would put up with all that now, no young person would let themselves be crushed in that way. I thought of going away, but really, where could I have gone? It wasn't easy in the thirties for a woman to leave home and start on her own, a woman in her thirties.

In the end mother really did become ill. She became senile rather prematurely. I felt sorry for her, not because she was my mother — she'd overplayed that years before. I felt nothing but coldness for her as a mother. I just felt sorry because she was an old woman and because old age comes to everyone. She had a stroke, and then became very dependent; and then she had a more serious stroke, and was bedridden for nearly two years before she died.

I think that was the worst period of my life. Going home, turning the corner of the street, looking at the house and wondering what I'd find. I used to go home at dinner time, and I'd always prepared the dinner, put a casserole in the oven, prepared the vegetables, so I could get her something to eat. And yet, every evening... how shall I describe the feeling of fear and anxiety when I turned that corner? What I might find? She could have fallen out of bed, she might have been taken ill and been unable to make anyone hear. For two years I was tormented by fear and yet hope. Hope that It might have happened. She might be dead, although I knew that when the time came, it would be not only a deliverance for me, but the beginning of an even more complete loneliness. I had no other relationship in the world. And I looked forward to it with terror, and curiosity at the same time. I wondered how I would survive. In a way I wanted it to come, because at least, then, I should know what it was like to be completely alone, I wouldn't be wondering about it all the time.

Eventually it did come. I was relieved, I felt very relaxed. I didn't cry when she died. I didn't rejoice either. I didn't feel anything at all. I looked at her dead, and thought how sad it had been, her life, and the way it had eaten up mine. She had been a cannibal, my mother.

I'd saved up out of earnings. I bought this house. I suppose I've thought about it a lot. She was so afraid of being lonely, she'd do anything to keep me with her; and I think I inherited the same fear, except that I didn't inflict it on another human being. If I'd had any really deep relationship, would I have preyed on him — or her, if I'd had a daughter? Perhaps it was a good thing I never entered into anything of my own making. As a matter of fact, my life is happier now than it's ever been. I have the occasional friend who comes to stay with me. We go to London even, to the theatre. I'm less lonely now than I've ever been. But that's because I don't expect anything from life now. Then of course I was young, and still had hope. I did expect things... I suppose I must be very bitter — I feel... extinguished. Do you think I'm bitter? I try not to inflict it on other people, even if I am bitter. People look at me and think 'What a nice old lady'. Am I though? If people only knew what you carry with you...

Miss Houghton did cry a little during the conversation; but afterwards she was quite composed and calm. I offered to call again, but she said that although she was quite happy to have told me everything, she would prefer not to see me again.

Stephen

Stephen is twenty-three. He is below average height, thin and self-effacing. He wears a plain grey suit with straight trousers, his hair in a page-boy cut. His gestures are nervous and his hands move a lot, as though they never know where to go next. He works in a department of the Co-Op as salesman, and he lives alone with his divorced mother in a terraced house half a mile from the centre of a Midland town. I taught him for a year in a secondary modern school in 1964. Since then, I have seen him from time to time, always alone. When he was at school he was unobtrusive, diligent and eager to please; the kind of child on whose report teachers write 'It is a pleasure to teach him.' Now he is isolated and introspective.

I think I've always been shy, but as I've got older it's worse. I'm afraid of people. I don't quite know what I'm afraid of. Sometimes I think 'Well what's the worst thing that could happen?' and then I realise, the worst thing they could do would be to hit me. But it still doesn't make any difference. When I'm at home, I feel I could talk to anybody. I can think of all sorts of things to say, but when I have to face people a kind of shutter comes down. I panic. I just want to run away from them. I just can't escape fast enough. And then sometimes I'll go home, and I could cry with feeling so miserable. I do sometimes. I sit in my room, and there's my mother downstairs with the television on, and she has it on loud because she's deaf. If I go in she looks at me and says 'Are you all right, dear?' And I smile, and she goes back to Police Five or whatever it is... She's so placid. I hate her sometimes. She never gets upset, she never argues. I want to say to her 'Why do you sit there like that, you know my life is all wrong, you know I have no friends, you know I can't get a girl-friend, why do you pretend everything's all right?'

My parents were divorced actually. She used to be quite violent with my father. He was very weak, scared of her. I used to listen to them late at night,

look down over the banisters when they were having
arguments. He used to get drunk — probably to get
away from her, and then she'd undress him and get
him to bed. She made out he was a real wrong 'un,
but he wasn't. She used to threaten that she'd put her
head in the gas-oven and take me with her, and write
a letter to the paper so that everybody knew why
she'd done it. They were divorced when I was twelve.
My father lives in lodgings; he's pathetic now. He
looks like a tramp, and he drinks. I know he's been in
and out of St. Crispin's [*the local psychiatric hospital*].
She always made out that he was irresponsible
and idle, but I think now that it was her really. She
just resented him. I don't know why. I don't know
what he'd done to her. I have these feelings of —
almost hate against her, and then I feel sorry about it
and try to make it up to her. She says, 'Don't soft
soap me.' She hates any show of feeling.

But she's the only person I have any real contact
with. Everything else is in my mind. Fantasy. If I've
met somebody — a girl, even if she's only a customer
I've seen in the shop, she's only got to smile and I
imagine all sorts of things that might happen. I go to
bed, and imagine that she might fall down or have an
accident, and I could be there and rescue her, and sit
by her bedside till she opened her eyes. It's silly I
know. But I look forward sometimes to going to bed,
so that I can think about things like that. I know it's
only fantasy, I know it's corny, but it's the only way
I keep sane. I never get my imagination mixed up
with reality. It's all I've got.

I'll tell you what makes me laugh. I saw some
people on television talking about the permissive
society. I thought Huh, I've never seen any sign of it;
and they were talking as if everybody jumped in and
out of bed all the while with the first person they
met, and the old lady said, 'Yes wasn't it shocking,'
and I said to her 'What the hell do you know about
it?' And she said 'I suppose you think it's all right, all
this VD, and doing things like dogs in the street.' I've
never been to bed with a woman. I've had two girl-
friends, but neither of them lasted long. One of them

worked in one of the other departments. I hadn't been going with her for more than a week, and she was talking about all the people she knew who'd got engaged. She didn't exactly propose to me, but I could tell the way her mind was working. She said things like 'Mick and Sue are getting engaged in November.' If I'd let her go on with it I'm sure I could have been married by now. She wasn't very attractive. No wonder so many marriages break up if people go into them the way Denise would've done. She didn't know me. She hadn't got the faintest idea of what was going on in my head. She said 'I do love you', and all sorts of things that couldn't possibly have been true.

At the time I really did feel lonely, but I think I'd rather stay alone than go into something for the sake of it. My own parents' experience was enough for me. She didn't even know me. I think perhaps I take a long time to get to know people, but once I do I'm very loyal. I don't like people who are suddenly all over each other, and then the next minute they've gone off with someone else. I don't suppose I'd have gone out with Denise, but her mate came and told me she liked the look of me. I don't know why. I'm nothing special. I've got a terrible inferiority complex. I used to imagine that everybody was looking at me wherever I went. Sometimes it used to be agony, even walking through the town. I used to blush even when people came into the shop; all the others used to chat with them and I could never think of anything to say. Funny really, sometimes I might pluck up courage and mutter 'It's a nice day', and they'd say 'Pardon' because I hadn't spoken loud enough, and then I said 'Nothing, it's all right', and they looked at me funny because they thought I'd made some personal remark about them. [*Laughs*] Actually I'm better than that now, I can say all the pleasant nothings that are expected, I'm quite good at it.

I get on quite well with the people I work with. It's funny how the people you see every day don't scare you, but those you don't know frighten you as much as ever. There's an old woman who's the cleaner, Dot, and she tells me everything about her life. She's sixty-eight. She says her husband sometimes still tries to get happy with her when he's had something to drink, and she says she keeps a pair of scissors under her pillow, and she says she'll use them if he tries anything on. Sixty-eight. She's lucky anybody still thinks about her in that way. She's very crude, but she talks to me. I like her, because I never have to provide the answers to anything she says. She'd talk to anybody.

I like people. I'd like to have friends. I go out for a drink sometimes with Graham from school. He's married now, but he has Friday night off [*grimaces*], and sometimes we go for a couple of pints. I've never been to a dance or a disco. I haven't got any sense of rhythm, I'm too self-conscious. In *Melody Maker* they advertise for spaced-out chicks, and groovy guys. I tell myself I could always answer one of those ads as a last resort. But then I think, if I did, they'd probably find I wasn't what they'd wanted, they'd say 'How dare you' or something like that. But then I think Well, there must be something the matter with them as well, or else they wouldn't need to put advertise-ments in the papers. I think you have to be very des-perate to do that. I don't know what I'd put in, even if I did, how would I describe myself 'Boring young man, 23, five foot ten, no O levels, likes sport, seeks beautiful intelligent girl with long blonde hair and a college education.' How many replies do you think I'd get to that?

I'm not stupid. I didn't do all that well at school. If you're shy, you just sit there and behave yourself and give no trouble. The teachers give all their attention to the troublemakers. They shout and rave. I used to really enjoy myself, looking at them, watch their false teeth move up and down when they got excited, or watch them spit in the air. On my report it always said 'Conduct excellent'. That's because they didn't even notice I was there. Story of my life, that is. That's what they'll put on my gravestone. 'Nobody noticed he was here'. Sometimes I wonder if I am. I'd like to do something to be remembered by, I don't know what. I wish I could write or something, like you do. That's the kind of thing I envy.

When I was younger, I wasn't all that bothered about being on my own. I've always been interested in sport. I didn't play much, but I used to go up to the County Ground and watch cricket in the summer, and take sandwiches, and I used to watch Wimbledon on the telly, I didn't know I was missing anything. My mother used to pack me up sandwiches so I could stay up at the cricket all day long. The sandwiches were horrible, and I used to throw them in the rubbish bin, but I loved sitting there in the sun, and I never minded being on my own. Some of the old men used to talk to me, and I liked that, because it was like old Dot in the shop: I never had to worry about making the right answer.

I earn twenty pounds a week now, take home sixteen, seventeen. I don't spend anything, apart from the five pounds I give the old lady. One year I went to Butlin's with my mate before he got married, but I hated it. The whole week was agony. I think he thought I was a bit of a drag. I've got quite a bit of money in the bank. I thought of buying a house, but what's the point? If I left the old lady, there'd be two lonely people in two houses instead of two lonely people in one house. If I could talk to her it wouldn't be so bad. She has no idea what my life is like. But she's always talking about me to the neighbours. She says I'm a bit of a lad, and some girl's going to be lucky, and he's good to his old Mum. Lies, all of it. I think she really believes it. Sometimes I go out for a drink on my own, just because of this fantastic social life she thinks I have. I go to a different pub every time, because if you go to the same one, people expect you to start conversations with them, and I can't. Sometimes, when I hear people talking, about sport, ordinary things I know quite a lot about, I'd really like to join in. But I just kind of pretend I'm not there, and hope nobody 'll notice me.

Once I went to the doctor. I was scared, and when he came to ask me what I'd gone for I said I had

earache, which was true. I thought he might find out

I was a real nutter, and lock me away and I'd never get out. I thought he'd think I was mad if I said I was lonely. Or he might have said 'Well what do you expect me to do about it, don't waste my time.' Do you think I ought to go to a psychiatrist? I do my job, I go home, I don't break the law, nobody notices me. Perhaps everbody's life is like mine underneath. But I know it isn't. When I go round town and see people together, not just people with girl-friends, but groups of lads together, families, they look happy, they've got company and I'm always on my own. I do cry sometimes. Two or three years ago I don't think I would ever have admitted it to anybody, but now I don't care. I don't even care what you think.

I saw Stephen again a few weeks after this conversation. He was anxious to stress that things were much better; that he had found himself a girl-friend, and was much happier. This may have been true, but he was slightly awkward and ashamed of having talked in the way he had done.

Mrs Skinner

Mrs Skinner lives in a new estate on the edge of a cathedral town in Southern England. She was a grocer in the Midlands during her working life. She was divorced twenty years ago, and her only daughter lives in New Zealand. She is a motherly and sad-faced woman of sixty-six, slow in her movements. She came here to retire and to forget a secret that she has borne all her life and that pursues her still; a secret she has never communicated to anyone.

When I got married, I think I just assumed that everybody was the same. It never occurred to me that people had different needs, or that some were more intelligent than others. I certainly didn't know that Joe was as ignorant and selfish as he was. And it took me years to find out. He was an attractive man in those days, good-looking — I'd never heard the word 'incompatible'. I knew that my own mother and father used to quarrel, but I always understood that was because he drank and there wasn't enough money left for food. What I never understood was that people have to get on together, that living with someone is the hardest thing in the world.

He came from the country, and was working as a slaughterman in an abattoir in the town where I lived. At the time I worked cooking the dinners for the men who worked there. He had a lovely smile, and he used to joke about my cooking, I really did fall for him. But he was just the same with any other girls he met, and I despaired of ever getting him. Then one day, he came into the kitchen, and he was dripping with blood over his apron. He said 'What's to stop us getting married?' Just like that. No preamble. He never courted me.

Well, we lived in two rooms for a little while, and I saved some money, as I'd always wanted to start up in business on my own. At first, he was going into road haulage with his brother, but they fell out over money, and he had to sell the lorry. Then we heard about these shops that had just opened on a new estate, which had just been built on the outskirts. So we talked it over, and we didn't have to put much down as a deposit. We found if he sold the lorry, with the bit we'd got saved, we could afford to stock it. It was very exciting. People moving into new houses, only ordinary people, people with a bit of ambition to do a bit better for themselves. They worked hard, and had a bit of money to spend, and there was no other shop in the area.

Of course, I realise now that things had gone wrong between us before we ever moved. In fact, I think I hoped that this would put things right. It meant I could pretend everything was all right. I don't think I was educated sexually. I suspected almost from the start he was seeing other women, although for a long time I had no evidence that this was the case, and if you care about someone, you always want to believe the best of them. But he spent money like water, and he liked to drink. I didn't mind him wanting a drink, but it got so that he wanted more and more before he'd be sociable. It was bad in the shop. One or two of the women we served were rather snooty, and if they could smell drink they used to take their custom elsewhere — there were one or two of the big grocers in town who used to deliver, so that didn't help matters.

He was supposed to do the rounds from the shop himself, but he was very slapdash, and sometimes he'd come back late at night with all the stuff he was supposed to deliver in the back of the van. And he took to going out at nights on his own, and not coming back till two or three in the morning. And then of course, he couldn't get up, and it was left to me to lug great sacks of potatoes about as well as do all the serving. In the end, I even did the delivery myself after the shop was closed. I took two wicker baskets, one on each arm, and I tramped the streets of that estate, sometimes till nine and ten at night. And I knew when I went rapping on people's doors at ten o'clock that they pitied me, because everybody but me knew what sort of a life he was leading.

I still wanted him, sexually, and at that time I still

enjoyed sexual relations with him. I knew he'd got this woman at home — in the village where his parents lived. Well I didn't know, but I'd got this shrewd idea, and anyway, somebody I knew said they'd seen him there on Saturday afternoons. Busiest time of the week in the shop that was. He always said he was going to the wholesalers, and looking round for places to buy more cheaply, but when he got back — sometimes not till Sunday dinner-time — and I asked him how he got on, he'd forgotten what he'd said he was going for in the first place. I was jealous, but I was also very foolish. I said to myself 'Well, as long as he comes back to me in the end I don't mind, I can take it.' I thought I'd show him how patient and forgiving I could be, and in the end he'd see how much more worthy I was than this wench he was seeing. It doesn't work out like that though, does it? People aren't attracted to those who love them, who do everything for them. They just take advantage of them. I was deluding myself.

Anyway, she gave him syphilis. By all accounts, she was a bit of an old — you know, a bit of an old whore. I didn't know, and nor did he for eighteen months or more. And then, even when he did know, he didn't tell me. When he went to the doctor, he even spun the doctor a yarn. Told him he thought he'd caught an infection from a rabbit. He used to go rabbiting a lot; he used to go poaching. That was the sort of people he came from, boozing and poaching; they were really terrible. Anyway, he said he reckoned he'd caught something from a rabbit. Oh he was devious. The first thing he ought to have done was tell me. I expect he thought I'd be so disgusted I'd walk out on him, and he didn't want that. He wanted the best of both worlds, as men do. Usually, anyway. I suppose there are exceptions. I've never met any of them.

If he'd told me then, I wouldn't have gone away. The business was just beginning to pick up a little. I was still having sexual relations with him occasionally, right up to that time. It's a miracle that I never caught it. And do you know how I found out?

My sister saw the van — we had an old van for the deliveries — parked outside the doctor's, and of course, he was going several times a week, and so she came and told me that I ought to know Joe was going to the doctor's several times a week, and that she had a good idea what was the matter with him. I don't know how she knew. But apparently this woman had a bit of a reputation, and I found out later that she was going for treatment at the same time, and someone Maud knew worked as an assistant to her doctor. It's funny how things get about.

Well I was flabbergasted. I asked him point-blank. One Saturday night I said 'Joe, is there anything the matter with you?' He put up such a performance, you've never heard anything like it. He said I'd been spying on him, made it sound as if I was in the wrong. But he had to admit it in the end. It was a terrible shock, I really felt sick. I didn't know what to do. I was thirty-four, I had no children. It was awful. I'd had a miscarriage a few years before, and I was rather ill, and after that we'd decided we didn't want children till we'd saved up a bit from the business. But as soon as I found out all that, I was aghast. I could see myself never having children at all. He moved into the spare bedroom, I couldn't have anything to do with him sexually when I knew that. But I looked to the future and I thought, well I can't leave him, not while he's as dreadfully ill as he is. Because at that time the illness really came out. It was terrible.

It was a funny thing, because a little while before all this happened, I'd got to know a man who was restoring the village church near where the estate was. And he'd come to the kitchen window one day and asked for some water for mixing cement or something, I don't remember exactly. But we'd got talking through the kitchen window. It was the time of the Jarrow marches, and he said something about it, and it turned out he was a socialist, and at that time I was a bit that way myself — I'm not now, I don't have faith in any of them — but we found we agreed on nearly everything. I could never have talked to Joe about such things, fond of him as I was. That's what

I meant, when I spoke about finding out about people when it's too late, and people being the same. I just didn't know there were people different from Joe. And this fellow had been to visit me once or twice, and I found I was pregnant.

Well you can imagine what a blow that was. I didn't know whether it was Joe's or Norman's. I went to the hospital, I had to have blood tests, and they said it was incredible that I hadn't caught anything from him. Naturally, I never said anything about Norman. Joe thought it was his. I told Norman everything. He said he'd help me financially, which he did, but apart from that, he didn't want to know. At the hospital, they said the baby would have to have a test as soon as it was born, but it was all right. Only how I got through the pregnancy I shall never know.

Joe was ill for two or three years. He'd got secondary syphilis, bordering on the third stage, and once it gets there, it's incurable. I can't describe what it was like, living with it. He had to have injections, arsenic, into his veins. Two or three times a week he had to go to the hospital. He had to have his own cup, his own knife and fork and plate, everything had to be kept separate. He wasn't allowed to touch the baby. It affected his nose and the roof of his mouth; all the time he was discharging, great endless streams of it. It collected in buckets that I used to take and empty down the drains. And he just lay on the settee for over a year. And the smell of it: it's haunted me ever since. I should know it wherever I was. If I was ever anywhere near somebody who'd got it, I should know.

I'd got Sheila, the baby, I was trying to run the business, and he was laying there in that terrible state. When Sheila was six weeks old, I got up one morning and decided I'd end it all. I knew exactly what I was going to do. I'd always hated water, I couldn't swim. I waited till after dark — it was April — and about half-past nine at night, I got my hat and coat on, and pushed her in the pram through the town, down to the river. I was walking very fast, and a lot of people looked at me. I suppose it was

strange to be wheeling a baby out at that hour. And I
got there — it was a good three mile walk — and I sat
on a bench. And I sat and sat. And I thought. Well
what right have I got to take her life away? I didn't
care a damn about my own. I don't care whether you
believe me or not. There she was, six weeks. I'd made
a hash of my life, but that was no reason to take hers.
And if I'd done away with myself, who would have
looked after her? Not Joe. And I'd said to myself for
years 'Oh, if only I had a child, I'll be all right, I'll be
able to put up with things.' There's nobody who'll
look after a child like the mother who's given it birth.

So I didn't do it. I went home. For a time I
thanked God for letting me live, but I damn soon
realised it was nothing to be thankful for. Joe
couldn't be allowed in the shop, not foodstuffs. He
couldn't go near anything, so I had all the work to
do. He couldn't work for some time. He just lay
there, looking at me, moaning and feeling sorry for
himself. Many a time I thought 'Arsenic, I'd give him
arsenic, the sod, but it wouldn't be in his veins.'
Terrible really. I didn't mean it. But he was so ill.
And I was afraid somebody might find out, and that
would ruin business. The disinfectant I used, I still
have the smell of it in my nostrils to this day. But he
got better in the end. It took all the roof of his
mouth away. I couldn't let Sheila go near him. I was
just revolted by him.

When he was better I divorced him. Not straight
away. I didn't expect gratitude from him. I stayed
with him out of duty, not out of love. He knew that.
He knew how I felt. But he took money from me, a
lot of money. When he was better, he started taking
women out in the town. He didn't make any secret of
it. Gossip soon got back to me, in the shop. He had a
lot of schemes. He was going to start building, he was
going to emigrate, he was going to London, he was
going to start in road haulage again. But nothing ever
came of any of it. I divorced him when Sheila was
seven. He got married again. They said it was
bigamous, the woman was married already. I don't
know whether it was true or not. He died of cancer

eight years ago.

I never told anyone except my sister, and she's dead. Sheila doesn't know. She's married. I don't know her husband very well, I don't even know if she's happy. Of course, I spoilt her, I over-protected her. And as she grew up, she resented it. I couldn't tell her why. But now all I've got to think about is all that, and wonder why it happened. When you're older you should have pleasant memories to look back on. Mine are all horrible, and even with time passing, it doesn't help. It wasn't an experience that you can take any pleasure in. I made up my mind Sheila would never know. She lives in New Zealand. Her husband is an engineer. I wonder if I shall leave it written down for when I'm dead.

I used to go and meet her father in town, once a week. Go for a drink with him, have a chat. He's dead now, died in a nursing home only two years ago. Isn't it funny, I was going to take my own life, and I've outlived them both.

Andrew Collison

*Andrew Collison, aged fifty-six, is one of those
archetypal successful and wealthy people, in whose
unhappiness the poor are said to find consolation for
their poverty. Barrister and company director, he
lives with his wife in a discreet Georgian house,
sheltered by the white hill-face of the South Downs,
and surrounded by dark beech woods. The drawing-
room is an assortment of muted peluche and velvet,
Regency stripes, an early Victorian escritoire in
golden walnut and an eighteenth-century chiffonnier.
Mr Collison is small and ascetic, with a pale and
rather cadaverous face. He was wearing a light grey
suit and a tie, although it was a warm afternoon.*

The trouble with me is that all my life I've hankered
after — not success, but appearing to be successful to
other people. I've lived in other people's judgments;
the outer trappings. It becomes a kind of captivity in
the end. I do conform: people have always said 'Oh
you've done all right for yourself; you've achieved
this; you flash past in your Lamborghini or whatever
motorised fad takes your fancy'; and you know they
admire you. It is very flattering. But it isn't important; it's all a substitute for something else. That is a
truth that sounds commonplace, but the experience
of it is quite the reverse I assure you. It is also heresy
in the circles where I move. You see, the pressures are
on me to maintain the pretence that my life is exem-
plary, a model to all those who are hardworking and
ambitious. But I'm a hostage to other people's con-
ceptions of achievement. I've never done what I really
want to do; and what's worse I no longer know what
that is. I've always felt, well I'm only working so that
I may earn my freedom to do what I please. And I
can't pretend any longer. I don't need to do anything,
but what I please. Only nothing pleases me.

I was born successful. My father was a bank
manager in Nottingham. I went to grammar school
and Oxford. My leg was badly broken when I was
thirteen, and it never grew properly after that, so I've

always had a slight limp. That is the only disadvantage under which I've ever laboured. I didn't have to go in the army. I've always been rather anti-militaristic as a matter of fact. But I started my life from the kind of base which it is other people's lifelong ambition to achieve. In a sense there's no way to go but up; and I was already half-way there. When I look at how effortlessly I've done what I have, well I'm slightly perturbed. I pretend I've had to fight and struggle, but I haven't really.

I always got on quite well with women, and when I married Caroline I chose a girl who would be a help to me in my career. That sounds rather harsh, but it didn't occur to me that she should have any other qualification, apart from being sexually attractive of course. I think I may be unnecessarily disparaging; at the time I was quite fond of her. I must have been. I can't recall what it felt like to be fond of her, it's a sort of distant memory. Our chief influence on each other was that we reinforced our pride. I've never known love. I can't see that I ever shall now. I sometimes get a feeling of panic. I can't believe that I'm fifty-six, and I've lost the chance, let alone the capacity, for a real love experience. Sometimes at night, I get this suffocating feeling of what's past, and I say to myself 'It's not true, I can't believe it, I shall wake up and find I'm twenty again, and I can see the trees of the courtyard of New College through the lattice window.' Then, when I get up in the morning, there's nothing but this terrible feeling of resentment. I resent everything that has brought me to this realisation. I resent my own upbringing, my parents who were obsessed with material standards, and I don't think they even realised how empty their own marriage was. They never slept together after I was born.

Do you know, the person I envy most of all in the world is my own son. He's twenty-two, and he's living with a girl in West London. He says he's a Buddhist, and goes in for this meditation business. He's a very nice boy, gentle. He's very tolerant, which is unusual in the young these days. We never had rows, even when he was living at home, although he used to say he was a Socialist, and that used to upset his mother. I was always rather amused, and a bit pleased with myself that I wasn't disapproving as so many parents are. But when he met Jane, and I saw them together a few times, then it really hurt me. I was pleased of course for him, but I could see at once that he had achieved something, at twenty-one, that I've never had and never shall. I'm jealous.

His mother says 'Isn't it frightful, isn't it ghastly,' and pretends to be all moral about it. It's her only defence of course; it's a mockery of what she calls standards, morals, decency. Of course our marriage is the greatest indecency of all. One thing I do know, it's painful to look back and realise you're mistaken, you've lived the wrong way, you've worked for the wrong things. I sometimes wonder if there are many people like me among those we know, but who can't admit it. I think there must be; only there's never a glimmer of it on the surface. We have too much at stake to admit it. They can't bear to admit there can be anything wrong with a society that gives them so much.

I have played with the idea of suicide, chiefly because of the effect it would have on the people who know me. People say 'Oh I know you', or 'Of course, you're this or that, you're a man of the world,' or 'You've had a lot of experience.' I'd like to shake that idea they have of me. I'd like to show that I'm as desperate and alone as it's possible for any man to be. I try not to be self-pitying. And I certainly don't have any time for those who say that being rich is more tragic than being poor. It bloody well isn't. Have you ever thought how few people actually admit to being rich? If they're rolling in money they say they're comfortable, if they're rich they plead poverty and if they're merely well off they say they haven't two halfpennies to rub together.

I can face that my life has been mistaken, only I haven't got the courage to do anything about it. And in any case, I feel guilty towards Caroline, because she's been part of the mistake and doesn't even see it.

She's discontented, she's not happy, but she hasn't the slightest idea why. She's on holiday in Morocco at the moment. She goes away three or four times a year. The last time I slept with her was in 1958, ten years after we'd been married. She blames me; she's not very intelligent, and has no capacity for abstraction at all. She feels that because we've led such irreproachable lives, she ought to be rewarded by happiness. She has the most absurd social formulae — worse things happen at sea, it wouldn't do for us all to be the same — things which she can't ever have examined the truth of.

She's very conventional; bridge and company entertaining and buying clothes are her principal delights. She's very attractive, five years younger than I am. She doesn't believe in adultery. She believes in marriage, even ours, God help her. I find her so remote from me that I don't bother to talk to her most of the time, except when people are there, and then we call each other darling all the while — the more trivial the remark, the more emphasis on the endearment: Another drink darling, are you cold darling, would you like to sit here darling. Then, when we're on our own, nothing. Mealtimes are the worst. We sit on either side of the table, and there's always a floral table decoration, and we talk like people who've just met in a hotel. But I wouldn't shatter her confidence in her life, even though I've none myself. I suppose I'm a coward. If I thought it could possibly do any good, I'd go away tomorrow. I'm quite good at my job, I like making money. I'd like to donate something to charity before I die. The Andrew Collison Memorial to loveless lives.

Alf

Alf is eighty-four. He lives with his son and daughter-in-law and their two children in a semi-detached house on the outskirts of Leeds. His own house was compulsorily purchased by the council two years ago, and he was paid nine hundred pounds for it. It is, he claims, the prospect of this money that prompts the humanitarian gesture of sheltering him in his son's home.

If I spend a penny of my money, Gladys goes mad. I bought a shirt, and she said 'What the heck do you want a new shirt for?' She could see a couple of quid being knocked off my few hundred. She thinks rags'll do for me. I shall only croak one of these mornings and leave them all behind. They watch me like hawks to see I don't fritter it away. I could quite enjoy it really, if I wasn't in the middle of it all. They are killing me off with their coldness.

[*Every afternoon Alf visits an old people's hut on the edge of the park. It is a wet afternoon in late October. The view from the windows is blurred by the streams of water smudging the panes. Inside the hut, there is a coal fire; dominoes, pipe tobacco, condensation, damp raincoats, smell of old age.*]

I come down here most afternoons. She locks the door on me from ten in the morning when she goes out to work till four o'clock when Darryl gets in from school. He's thirteen. He can be trusted with a front door key, but I can't. They give me my bit of grub. I've got a warm bed. But they don't care. They're indifferent. They never talk to me, never ask me what I think. I've got no business to be thinking at eighty-four. Glad talks to the dog with more affection in her voice than I ever get. If she knew what was going through my mind sometimes, she'd have a fit. It's a very funny thing, but I'm in the same position now that I've always been, all my life. I've never been able to speak my mind.

My mother died having me. They never thought I'd live. My sister told me years later they were so upset with mother dying they forgot all about me. Apparently she took pity on me and said 'We might as well let him die in the warm,' and they put me on a chair in front of the fire, and that revived me. I didn't have a happy childhood. I had a stepmother who was very unkind. My father was getting on when I was born. He'd been in the Crimea, and he could remember them bringing all the wounded in and sawing off their arms and legs without any anaesthetic. And when they got to the marrow like, in the bones, they said they screamed and shouted terrible. He was a sick man himself, so he sent me to his sister's in Norwich. She had no time for me. I was a skivvy there. I was. No better than a skivvy. She let me know every crust of bread I ate was given out of charity, because my father was dying. She wouldn't let me go back home. One day, she went out and left me with a neighbour. She was all in black. When she came home, she took off her gloves and said 'We've just buried your father.'

I went to work in the fields. I remember working by moonlight. Harvest time, we worked carrying by moonlight. When the war started I was in my twenties, I was still living with her. It never occurred to me to up and go. But I went to the war. On the Somme. I saw some terrible things; men shot to pieces. I thought then it was the most wicked war there's ever been, but you couldn't say so. You wouldn't have dared.

I got married in 1919. I never liked her much, and I don't like her son. He's just like her. I sometimes wonder if he's mine at all. But you're stuck with them, aren't you? You can't choose your own flesh and blood. Pity. The trouble with me is I see too much in people. I see too much but I'm not allowed to open my mouth.

Mrs Calthorpe

Mrs Calthorpe is forty-three years old. She earns about L10 a week as an office cleaner and receives family income supplement. She is living temporarily in one of the last occupied houses in a clearance area in the centre of a Northern town. Her husband is in prison, not for the first time, for a series of attacks on women, including a rape, and she is left with four children between the ages of eight and sixteen. The street is littered with fragments of broken glass, so that it is virtually impossible to walk without crunching splinters of glass underfoot. Mrs Calthorpe says it's a death-trap for the younger children, who are always coming home with cuts and gashes. Apart from that, vagrants have removed the pieces of zinc from the boarded-up windows, and this allows rats to escape into the street. In the back garden the grass is high and rank; the garden wall has collapsed in several places, so there are heaps of red bricks at intervals. There is a sofa in the middle of the yard, which Mrs Calthorpe says came from the Welfare and proved to be infested.

The interior of the house is shabby and fetid. A dog, almost devoid of fur, sleeps under an old coat in the corner. There is a blazing fire, although the day is warm, and a bag of coal stands beside the grate. Mrs Calthorpe wears no make-up, and looks pale and drawn. She wears a stained pink sweater and a navy-blue short skirt. She has no stockings, and her legs are pale, with the veins standing out, blue and knotted.

Why should I be punished, just because I happen to be his wife? I'm not punished like he is, once; I'm punished every day. Every time I go round to the shops, there's somebody's tongue going. 'Here she comes.' I've heard them say it. He's doing time. It all reflects on me. Anybody would think I'd made him go out and do it, the way they talk. He's supposed to have raped this girl. They say he raped her, but if he did, he raped her screaming for it. Everybody knows her. She's been hanging round the Cherry Tree —

that's the pub where all the old prosses go — and she's
been going down there since she was about thirteen.
I'm not exaggerating. I could kill her, she's a little
bitch. She's lived for years in a children's home,
though she must be about seventeen by now.

She's got a flat with another girl just as bad. They
don't have any proper control over her, she's allowed
to do just what she likes. I know she's been round the
town for several years, because I've seen her myself in
pubs. She was walking through the park — or so she
said — one night last October. Girls of seventeen
going through parks on their own — they're only
looking for one thing. They hadn't got any proof it
was him. Just because he'd had convictions years ago,
it still follows you. You can't get away from it. They
came and picked him up the next night. He did go
with her, but he said she asked him to. They said he
followed her out of the pub, and into the park. She
could've done it and then decided she'd get him into
trouble — tear her clothes a bit, scratch her face or
whatever it was she said he'd done to her.

But you see if he goes with a girl like that how
does it make me look? I get it all back at me. It makes
me look as if I ain't good enough for him. I can't go
and tell all these people tattling about me what the
truth is. I've had him here, crying like a baby, holding
on to me, saying 'Help me, help me'. I might as well
tell you, I don't care anyway. He's always been over-
sexed. He has to have a lot of sex, he says he has to. I
know it's true. He says he has to have it all the time.
It's been going on for years. I told him, as long as I
don't see you doing it, and as long as they don't all
know about it round here, I don't care what goes on.
I've shielded him before.

You know what happened only last Christmas? We
had such a performance. Terry — he's my oldest boy,
he's married now — he was sitting here, on that
settee, with Tricia, his girl-friend. I was out the back
doing something. Anyway, Terry's mate came rapping
at the door; somebody had pinched his car or something, I don't know what it was all about. While
Tricia was on her own in the room, he comes in, and

evidently sits down the side of her. She said she thought it was funny at the time, I mean, there was nobody else in the room, so why did he have to go and sit there? There was plenty of other chairs. He picks up a newspaper and then a few minutes later, Trish says she feels him up her thighs, all warm. He gets her and tells her to sit still or he'll strangle her. I'm in the kitchen, don't know a thing about it. Anyhow, she screams, and he's got her by the throat. I come running in — she was white as paper, all shaking and trembling. Terry comes in and says he'll leather him, but I wouldn't have that. I said 'No, we shall have to go to the police.' Of course, he denied it. He always does. He says, innocent-like, 'What are you going on about, I never done a thing, me zip just bust.' I don't know how he's got the face to sit there and lie like that. We saw him. I saw him, and Trish saw him, poor little gal.

But I've known how he's been for years. He's come and boasted to me about all the women he's been with. I said to them, 'I've always said I don't care, so long as I don't catch him at it in this house.' I didn't know what to do, because he'd never done anything like that in here before. I've always had to be careful, though. The girls didn't dare get up in the night, not even to go to the toilet, because he might be there, floating about with nothing on. I mean, nothing's ever happened, not with me being here, but Christ knows, if I hadn't kept my eyes open. When it brings other people into it like Tricia, I feel terrible, then. Tricia was ever so nice over it, but she could've turned awkward; a lot of girls would have done. You don't expect that sort of thing, not when you go round your boy-friend's house for a Christmas drink.

That's what I've been living with for the last twenty years. Now it's all come out, I feel worse if anything. It was all for nothing, shielding him. I don't know why I bothered. I suppose I'll be here waiting for him when he comes out. But why should I have to suffer for it? It's not only the clacking that goes on, I can stand that. There's all sorts of other things. Men think they've got a right to leer up to you and start propositioning you. I've stood at bus-stops and had them say to me 'I bet you're lonely at nights'. 'Not for you', I said to him. He was horrible. But I daresay I could, if I let myself. Then there's the Social Security. I get ten quid a week. I've been bad. I was laid up in the spring with ulcers. I have to be careful what I eat. You go to them for a bit extra; they cross-question you; they want to know more about you than you know yourself. He said 'Had I got a man living with me?' I turned round and said 'Only if you want to move in, love.'

I feel empty since he went. It's a bloody shame. And that bloody bitch, walking about scot-free. I'm the one who's punished most. There's Linda at school; all the kids know. The whole town knows. Because he's not crooked. He'd worked for the same firm for seven years; they gave him ever such a good character. He could've mixed with a real load of crooks where we used to live, but he wouldn't have a thing to do with them. They said he had to have medical reports. He's not unbalanced, he's not crackers. He's clever. He can paint, he can draw beautiful. It all seems senseless.

Mrs Webb

A September evening in a small terraced house on the edge of a small town. The interior is well-worn and comfortable—plaid rugs, cut moquette, chunky china ornaments, photographs; a work-box with a tangle of coloured lengths of wool. Mrs Webb, a retired domestic servant of seventy-seven, is warm, industrious and thrifty, with a slight disability which makes it difficult for her to walk very far. Twice a week she goes to a Centre for the Disabled and Elderly, and on Sunday she meets three widows who, like herself, struggle to keep at bay the desolation of being old and childless.

I've always been the kind of person who is rather apart. Even as a child. I was brought up in the country, in a tied cottage on a farm. My father was the cowman, and next door lived the horseman. He wasn't my real father, because my mother married again when her first husband died, and he had three children already. So I was the outsider, never quite part of them. I felt they always had secrets from me. I was on my own a lot, although I always loved the countryside. I remember the woods near us, a carpet of bluebells in the spring; and in the autumn there was blackberrying and mushrooming. It's strange really, I've grown nearer to my brothers and sisters as I've got older than I ever was as a child. I'm going to stay with my sister for a few days. She's just lost her husband, and she can't stand being on her own.

I left school when I was twelve and I had to go into service. I went to a young couple who were farmers, and I had to live in. It was about fifteen miles from home and it seemed to me the back of beyond. It was big rambling place, and I was the only help they had. I got one and threepence a week. They weren't bad to me, but they used to go out a lot and I'd be in the place on my own. I'd go and look in all the cupboards, under beds, I was literally terrified. I helped the mistress make butter, and sometimes I used to milk the cows as well. Anyway, I didn't last long. I

got so lonely. I went to a butcher's wife near Welling-
borough. She was a terror. There was another maid
there, and fortunately we got on well together. We
could laugh and cover up for each other if we did
anything wrong. We slept in an attic, and we had to
be up at six o'clock in the morning. If we were a
minute or two late, she'd be there and want to know
why. I reckon she laid awake all night long, just for the
pleasure of catching us out in the morning.

I had fifteen places in twelve years, and only at one
of them was I treated like a human being. They didn't
think of us as people like themselves. We were different. Occasionally my father and brother used to come
and see me, and I felt really unhappy when they left.
I wanted to say 'Take me away with you', but of
course they couldn't. You had to work; your parents
couldn't afford to keep you. Sometimes, if I'd been
home, when the time came for me to go back I used
to pray that the train wouldn't come or that it would
crash. But it always came.

Then I went to a doctor's wife. She was dreadfully
unkind. I had one day off a month, a Sunday, and the
other general had the same. One day I heard her
telling her friends she always had a big party on the
Sundays the maids worked — never on their days off
because she'd have had to do too much work herself.
I had to serve at table as well, so I never ate a meal in
peace. I'd no sooner sit down than the bell would
start ringing to clear away their first course and start
on the pudding, so by the time I got back to my own
it was stone cold. Sometimes she used to stand over
me while I ate, and taunt me. 'Is that all you can do,
fill that fat stomach of yours?' Once she caught me
writing a letter home at half past six in the evening,
and she came in and said 'I don't pay you to sit here
and write letters.' And I'd been working since six in
the morning. Oh, I went to some terrible places. Anyway, in the end I must have given her some backchat,
because I was dismissed. Of course, you were always
worried, because if they dismissed you they wouldn't
give you a character. It's funny, our employers always
demanded a character from us, but we were never

allowed to ask for a character from them before we
went to work there. I often wondered what they
would have said if we'd asked for one.

I've been married twice. I met my first husband
when he was home on leave from the Great War. We
were married in Lowick church. It's a beautiful place,
a lantern tower and some glass hundreds of years old.
Anyway, he was gassed and he had dysentery, and he
was never really well after that. A lot of the time he
couldn't work at all. Some of the time I used to
work, domestic help like. I had to go to the Assistance Board. They sat there and cross-questioned
you, and then muttered among themselves, and then
they might let you have a few shillings. It was
humiliating. In the end, I got a cottage in the country, near where I was brought up. I thought 'Get him
into the fresh air, he'll be better there.' I thought he
might be able to do a bit of agricultural work, but he
couldn't. We moved in the February, and he died in
the August. I was a widow for eighteen years. My
brothers and sisters still lived in the same village. I
used to see them go past my window two or three
times a week, but they never came in to see me.
Occasionally on Sundays, at Christmas, I used to go
to tea, that's all. We were never close.

Ten years ago I went on a holiday for the elderly,
and that's where I met my second husband. I met him
at a whist drive. I'd met him before as a matter of
fact, on the same kind of holiday, but hadn't had
much conversation with him. He said he wanted a
housekeeper, and would I be interested. I said 'Oh
no.' 'Well,' he said, 'Come and see the house anyway.
I'd like to see you.' So I did, and we arranged to meet
again. We got on, and in the end we decided to get
married. I had seven years of real happiness. I've had
my share of happiness. I don't know, do you think
you have to pay for the happiness you have? Do you
think you have to give it back in sorrow? But beneath
it all there's always been this feeling of being different. I've no children for one thing, and that makes a
difference.

59   [*A neighbour calls with an open wooden box full*

*of fresh runner beans from the allotments behind
the terrace.*] I'm going to salt these down for the winter.
You lay them in salt, they'll keep all right till Christmas. Lovely beans. Of course, they always taste a bit
salty, but it's nice to have fresh vegetables in the
middle of winter.

I worry about what to do with this house. The roof
needs seeing to, but I don't use the upstairs at all. I'm
afraid of having a fall. I've got my bed in the front
room, so there's two bedrooms upstairs not used. I
wonder if I should get my name down for a council
flat, but you hear of so many cases of people being
moved and then not being happy. Some of them give
up the ghost when they're shifted out of their own
little home. I can do as I like here, my bit of shopping
and cooking. I go to a day centre twice a week, and I
love that. I've arthritis, but as long as I can still get
about I'd rather stay here. Do you think it's best? I
do.

*September twilight; a pale sunset against the
window. Mrs Webb's face is dark and sad in outline.
Her shoulders are rounded, her hands lie in her lap.
The clock ticks ponderously. For a moment I sense
what it is like to be old: not simply failing strength,
and a life bounded progressively by the street, the
front doorstep, the armchair and the bed, but to be
burdened with a weight of social experience as well;
to have known things that no one will ever live
through again.*

Martin

Martin is a vagrant. He is twenty-four years old and has no income. Somewhere in South London he has a mother and a large family of brothers and sisters. He is tall with dark hair and an impassive, fleshy face. He wears a tee-shirt and jeans and short jacket. His brown suede boots are shabby and splashed with dried mud. It is not immediately obvious that he sleeps rough. He manages to keep himself just clean enough to be attractive, and this is important for his survival. Most nights he sleeps out in London. In summer it's easy; the nights are warm, and even if the parks are locked, he has no difficulty getting into them. Occasionally he goes to Salvation Army hostels, or other hostels for homeless single men, and the cost of this is borne by the Social Security. At other times he receives nothing from Social Security, because they insist on an address before they will make any payment. He will sometimes beg, sometimes take money from newspaper stands, occasionally steal from houses if they look especially tempting and unattended. He goes to homosexual bars—not often, because he doesn't want to become too well-known, and is sometimes picked up and taken to people's flats or houses. These moments of luxury seldom last long, because he isn't homosexual, and his protectors soon tire of him. Once he met an elderly man who kept him for nothing in a flat in Victoria for nearly two months. From time to time he runs into people who have taken him into their homes at some time, and, embarrassed, they offer him two or three pounds and make their escape.

Martin came from Ireland when he was five, the third of eight children. They lived in rooms, basements, flats, all over South London, and he spent two periods in a 'Council home,' when his mother disappeared without warning and went back to Ireland. When Martin was fifteen, his father was seriously injured on a building site, and has not worked since. Martin worked at first—hodman, fruit-picking, dust-bin man for Lambeth Council, van-driver's mate, warehouseman—although none

*of these jobs lasted for more than four or five
months. Now he no longer works at all; a position
which he justifies by saying 'I saw what happened to
my old man; I don't want to finish up with a hole in
my head.'*

*He is indignant and sentimental about those who
sleep out on the Embankment, around the stations, in
the hostels; and he blames 'tourists' for the lack of
accommodation for the poor, the building of hotels
instead of homes. Since he has always lived among
the deprived and outcast, he has the impression that
they outnumber those who live in houses and lead
'respectable' lives. And yet he still borrows from the
culture that has failed him, the images of his self-
esteem. He likes to think he is strong and courageous
and he imagines he'd like to join the army, but they
wouldn't have him because he's colour blind. He
boasts that there must be five or six birds walking
round the West End who are carrying his kids. He
went to a 'backward' school, but he said they taught
him nothing. 'I had to learn to read and write when I
left school,' he explains, but he didn't know he was in
the Walworth Road, although the name was on a
plaque behind the bench where we were sitting. He
likes to think of himself as liberated, picaresque,
free-booting; he takes on a gang single-handed who
are attacking an old man, and they flee; he'd kill
anybody he saw tormenting animals. He despises the
people who do the same job year in year out.*

It'd drive me mad. I couldn't work indoors. I feel I
can't breathe in a factory. I don't like being indoors
at all. If I wanted to be indoors I could go home. We
lived over a funeral shop. The old lady told us they
kept the bodies downstairs, and if we did anything
bad they'd come out of their boxes. My oldest
brother, he was a right villain, he took one of the cars
and crashed it over Battersea Bridge. They sent him
to Borstal, and we had to move. Brixton. Jungle
drums. I don't mind them, as long as they leave me
alone, but if they try anything I'll smash them. I
ought to have been a boxer. They wanted me to at

school. I could have had professional class, but I had this girl, and she said it'd spoil my looks. I've still kept my looks. People said I was good-looking. Do you think I'm good-looking? What would you say if you saw me in the street? I know I haven't got long left. I'm twenty-four. If I don't make up my mind what I'm going to do, it'll be too late. I look after myself though. It does you good, being out in the open. It's more healthy. I never have a cold. When I lived at home I always had colds. That's why I hate factories. All that dust in your lungs. They never live long in factories, they're all dead by forty, most of them. When we lived over the funeral shop, they were nearly all people who'd been in factories.

I ought to have got married. I had this girl called Mary. She wanted to get married, but we would've had to go and live with her Mum and Dad. I might've settled down then. But I used to go with other girls and she didn't like it. I think the best times were when I was on the buildings. All these women used to go by; they stopped and looked you up and down and said 'I bet you know where to put it', — practically asking you for it. You could have any of them. They used to be there with prams, kids, you know, to make out they were just walking by. You used to get to know them, the same ones were there all the time. I had more women then than I've had since.

I like a drink. I used to spend all my money on drink. When I was on the buildings, I used to get thirty quid a week. I'd have six or seven meals a day and drink twelve pints. If you eat a lot with it, it doesn't do you any harm. I used to go into a café, eat eggs and bacon six times a day. I don't eat much now. You can follow the soup round at night, half a dozen places, if you know where it's going. Charing Cross, then it goes to the Embankment, then King's Cross, Stepney. If you follow it, you can get six or seven lots. I do if I'm hungry, but it's a long way to walk. I drink more than I eat really. Some of these dossers, they drink anything, meths. You don't last long once you've started on meths, a few months and you've had it. Car battery juice, they'll try anything with alcohol in it. Sometimes I wake up in the morning, I'm shaking till I've had something to drink. Then I'm all right. Look at my hand, if I stretch it out like that, I can't keep it still. I shall be all right when I've had a couple of pints. I don't like drugs, though. I think they're wrong. Some of these blokes I've seen, their arms are all swollen, poisoned where they've put the needle in. You must be mad to do that.

I don't want to get old. Thirty-five'll be enough for me. I believe in God and I believe in the devil. I think they're the same thing. I wonder what happens to you when you die? I think you just die and that's that.

North Camberwell Open Space. Some wooden benches, a low wall, beds of yellow and red hybrid tea-roses. Under the bench some discarded cider bottles. On the bench next to where Martin and I are sitting, there is a woman with loose grey hair, a battered herring-bone tweed coat, with a dog and a bundle in a pram. She is fondling a man in his forties, unshaven, torn grey flannels, sports coat, no shirt. The passers-by look at them from a distance, but look away as they draw level. A bus stops at the traffic lights; a row of pink smudges at the window turn in unison.

Mrs Douglas

Mrs Douglas is the widow of a labourer in her mid-sixties. She lives in a terraced house in a village and her income is from Social Security.

It was terrible the way my husband died. He'd not felt well for a long time, he'd a pain in the chest, and he thought it was indigestion. He went to the doctor's, and got something for it, but it didn't go, and in the end they sent him for an X-ray. They said he'd got a small growth in his chest, not very big. They said he'd have to go into hospital. Well he didn't want to go, but he did in the end. I went in to see him on the Thursday afternoon before he was due to have the operation. And I came home, and I was in the kitchen peeling potatoes, and all of a sudden the door opened and there he was. He'd got scared and run away; just got dressed and walked out.

Anyway, we talked it over, and he talked it over with the children, and they all said he must make his own decision, and in the end he said he would. He agreed to go back and have the op. Well it was all right, he got through that, only they took his whole lung away. I think he had cancer. But we saw him the day after, and he looked all right. He was at Oxford and the children drove me over in the car. And we went to see him again on the Sunday and he'd had a stroke. Oh, he looked terrible. He couldn't speak. He just lay there, and his eyes were wide open, and he seemed to be begging me to take him away from there. Oh, it did upset me. I thought afterwards he looked like a man who'd seen something so shocking he couldn't talk about it. I cried all the way home. And then of course, the next morning there was a policeman at the door to say he'd died. And I blame myself. If I'd said to him not to have the operation, perhaps he wouldn't have died. I don't know. If it was only a small growth. Or perhaps that's only what they tell you. When he walked out, perhaps he did it for a reason, perhaps he knew he wouldn't survive it. I've thought about it and wondered and wondered....

I was over forty when we got married. He was a widower then, with five children. When he died his family wanted him to lie with his first wife, and they came to see me and asked me if I'd mind, and I said 'Well no, I'd rather be cremated when I die, I don't want to be buried', so I didn't mind. And they buried him in the churchyard, with his first wife. Only a few days later they discovered that they'd made a mistake, they'd missed the grave, they'd put him in the wrong place. They had to dig him up and re-inter him in the proper place. That was terrible, to have to go through another ceremony the week afterwards. You thought it was all over and there we were going through it all over again.

This room seemed enormous after he died, it seemed empty. The house seemed vast, I used to sit in a corner of it. The evenings are the worst, Sundays especially. I wrote to Shelter, saying I'd got a home I'd share with someone, preferably an older person, a lady my own age, but they wrote back and said it was families they wanted accommodation for. I miss companionship. You can't hold conversations with the television. Quite often I do, as a matter of fact. When they're arguing I say 'What rubbish'. I feel I could put things as well as they do, the experts and that, and I carry on a conversation with them, although I suppose it sounds a bit silly. Exchanging arguments with the television, that's what I call being lonely.

Norman
Blake

*Norman Blake is a retired shopkeeper of sixty-one
who lives off his savings and modest investments.
For the past three years he has lived in a privately-
rented flat in a southern market town.*

Even today I tremble with secret anger, and I'm
over sixty, when I think of my first twenty years,
which were completely empty of love and affection,
and especially of parental love. Those two decades
have haunted me, because they forced me to live an
abnormal life.

My birthplace was Stoke-on-Trent, where my
maternal grandfather owned a small pottery business.
My mother was the youngest of his family of seven,
and I was born to her when she was nineteen. Because
I was an illegitimate child, my unwelcome appearance
threatened a public scandal.

So, presumably on the orders of my Puritan grandfather, soon after my birth I was whisked out of the
family mansion secretly, and taken north to Manchester, where an elderly Welsh couple had been paid
to adopt me. When I was sent to school at the age of
five as 'Norman Chettle', I didn't know that it was
not my real name. I was eighteen when I learned the
truth about my parentage, and I lived until then without any real identity.

Now, in late middle-age, I know that I was an unwanted child, a rejected child, someone with an 'unknown father', and probably rejected in the womb
even before birth. I began this life of mine without
parents, and was forced to live for many years in a
state of hopeless isolation.

As a young man I realised that my whole personality had been twisted because my soul had been
starved of love, so I have never felt like a real, inte-
grated human being. During those vital developing
years, I seemed to live outside the human race,
lonely, not sharing, and not knowing why I had to
carry this burden.

There was one awful thing about my situation —

I'd been adopted by a family who didn't really want a child in their midst. They were too old. The Chettles had had a family, now mainly dispersed, and at their age simply weren't interested in children any more. It was not surprising that they neglected me and didn't show any interest in my welfare. My foster-father was a barber, at first self-employed, and later he opened a small shop in a slum street on the edge of Cheetham Hill, the Jewish district of Manchester. We lived above, and at the back of the shop. I must have been six or seven when I began to understand that I was an outsider, and that I didn't belong in that house. IT WAS NOT MY HOME. 'Father' Chettle began to speak quite openly at meals about my alien origins, and teased me about being a tiny baby when I was brought to them. After that, I always felt that everyone else was stronger than I was: I was an intruder, I had no right to be there.

Now that I knew the Chettles were not my real parents, I secretly began to wonder who my mother was, but I never thought about my missing father. I was a silent child, withdrawn, thinking my own thoughts, so I never questioned them about my real parents. Although the house was filled with violence, Celtic violence, because the old man was so often drunk, they did not beat me or ill-treat me. They were just indifferent, and gave me a minimum of attention. I was allowed to run wild in those slum streets, and that freedom left me with an anarchistic yearning all my life.

When I learned that I was 'no one', I slowly began to feel that particular quality of personal loneliness that has filled my life. Although there was plenty of life in the street outside, noise from the customers who came into the shop, I simply felt separate from them all. I became obsessed with wondering: where did I belong? Where were my own people? When I look back at my early years I realise that most of all I missed what children need above everything — touch. For me there were no kisses, no hugging, no warm embraces and no loving caresses. I never touched another child and no one ever touched me. I lived within myself. Something had happened to my emotions: I seemed to be frozen, despite the fact that I was an imaginative child with a precocious and active brain.

My loneliness got worse as I grew older. The Chettles started going out at night, leaving me alone, not in the house, but in the dark street. I had to stay there till they returned, sometimes late at night. Other children ran home to their parents. I hated the dark, and I have always hated the darkness, which intensifies my 'shut out' feeling. I would try to huddle near to the door of a pub or lean against the lighted window of a small sweet-shop. During those lonely night hours, which still haunt me today, I would feel 'different', and wonder why I didn't belong.

Then there was something which at the time seemed even worse. I was not only starved of mother love, but, just as vital, I was also starved of actual food. We never had enough to eat. I was always hungry; and it wasn't until late in my youth that I could look at food without wanting it. I ate at the family table, which included their young daughter Emily, who worked at a local biscuit works. It wasn't that they denied me anything — I shared what they had; only it was so little. Sometimes things got very bad and we were reduced to bread and margarine. I suppose the old man spent too much on drink. Sometimes there was no money in the house at all, and we had to wait till he brought some home. Lack of food at that age meant that I began with a poor physical foundation, and it certainly had a bad effect on my physique. My bones lacked calcium, especially my legs, which have always suffered from malnutrition.

I had turned seven when my life with the Chettle family ended: my foster-mother died suddenly in hospital. This meek woman had never been unkind to me, but had looked after me in a rather indifferent fashion. I broke down at the funeral and cried. I don't remember ever crying before then, and it made a deep impression on me.

The death of Mrs Chettle brought a crisis in my

young life. What were they to do with me now? There was no one to look after me — old Chettle and Emily were hopeless. They didn't want to keep me anyway. It was the same old story: no one wanted me. I had not been welcome in Stoke-on-Trent; I wasn't wanted in Manchester. Was there anywhere in the world where I could feel I belonged? By this time I was fully conscious of what was happening. There was a family council after the funeral, and all the Chettles gathered there decided that I must be returned to the Blake family in Stoke, my own family.

In a few days the Chettle sisters, three of them, took me to Stoke and told the Blakes that they must have me back. I was forced to sit in a small room in the Blake mansion while the sisters argued their case; and I sat and listened to the stormy scene, the raised feminine voices in the next room. At that moment, even at that age, I became aware of the whole horror of human existence. All through the next decade I remembered that scene, and I could not wipe it out of my thoughts.

But before my fate was settled, I had to go back to Manchester, where I was put in the charge of some strange widow for a week. Then I was collected by one of the older Chettle sisters who took me by train down to the South of England, to Hampshire, to the cathedral town of Winchester. I had no idea why we were making that long journey, but I feel I shall remember it until the end of time. That cold day ended my brief childhood: it had been a loveless time, filled with dreaming loneliness. Now came the moment when the human spirit triumphed in me: I wanted to live, to live and survive.

I wasn't then fully aware of my problem. I didn't understand that the total and disastrous lack of love in my childhood was the most vital determinant in my character. It was the key to the whole strange course of my emotional and sexual life as an adult. That understanding came later, much later.

On that winter night I began a new life in a small bungalow on the outskirts of Winchester. It was to be a lower middle-class life, with proper living and

enough food, with discipline, but again completely
without love. So that my boyhood and youth were
also spent in a 'casa senza amore'. Now I found myself living with a family called Wood. But this time I
didn't take their name; my new name was Norman
Blake, my real family name.

The youngish woman of the house was described as
my 'aunt' and her husband as my 'uncle'. They had a
son about my own age who was my 'cousin'. There
were two great compensations in my new life. So far I
had been a real townee, but now I came into contact
with the real green country. Hampshire couldn't have
been a greater contrast to the Black Country of my
birth. Now that I was moving out of infant class, I
began to love going to school. I liked the atmosphere,
I liked learning, and I liked all the teachers; and the
men teachers especially seemed to be superior beings.
They were kind to me, because I was intelligent and
looked up to them. When I went to that Winchester
school, an ordinary school for working-class boys, I
suddenly seemed to change. I became a compulsory
chatter-box; as though all the years of silence and
repression had to burst forth. I was caned all the time
for the crime of not keeping silent, but I felt no resentment. This completely changed atmosphere must
have had some effect upon my character.

But both at home and outside the home I still remained shy and withdrawn, because I felt I was still
living with strangers, despite the claim of the blood-
tie between us. The atmosphere was still cold and
loveless. I was given the impression that this family
was related to the Blakes, but I failed to understand
the relationship. That is, until we went to visit my
real grandparents in Stoke-on-Trent. There I met
grandfather Blake, a dignified, good-looking old man
with a silver beard. Grandmother Blake spent most of
her time in bed, surrounded by medicines.

Surrounded by real relatives, I now began to puzzle
about their exact relationship to me. One of the
Blake sons or one of the Blake daughters must have
belonged to me. Which one? I couldn't work it out,
because I didn't feel related to anyone there. I never

dreamed that I was actually living with my own flesh and blood mother.

One year after my birth, she had married a young Hampshire builder she had met on holiday; and she probably hoped that Norman, the first child of her womb, would never appear again. Now that I had annoyingly turned up a second time, they made the best of a bad job and took me in as an 'orphan'. The result of this was that I lived in Winchester as much a stranger as I had done in Manchester. I was in a severely respectable atmosphere, and was desperately unhappy all the time I was growing up.

All through those years my mother seemed to hate me, and she treated me like some wicked child delinquent, whereas she doted on Oswald, for whom nothing but the best was good enough. There were times when I felt that I must be filled with the spirit of the Devil, I was so tortured. I was being punished for existing, and because I was a living reproach to her past wrongdoing.

When I was about twelve, she started making me do quite a lot of housework. As Oswald didn't do anything because he was studying, I felt that I was some sort of inferior being in that house, and I bitterly resented those household chores. There was no way in which I could revolt. There was nowhere to go. When I was still a schoolboy I did try to run away but I didn't get far. The police picked me up and sent me back to Winchester.

For years I had to get up early to light the coal fire for breakfast in the kitchen. When I happened to oversleep — natural enough in a growing boy — my 'uncle' would come into the room and beat me savagely with a slipper, or even a stick. I never forgave him. When he died, I refused to look at him in his coffin. I felt that he had committed a sin against the Holy Ghost.

I was a slim fifteen when I left school where I had been happy, and I went to work in a small electrical factory on the other side of the town. That meant travelling, taking my lunch, being away from home. At least I was among men who knew nothing about me. All the time I pondered the problem of escape, for I knew I had to leave that domestic hell sooner or later. But I wasn't yet earning enough money for the move.

After a violent row when I was just sixteen I managed this time to run away as far as London. But I did a stupid thing — I travelled on the London train without buying a ticket, and when the ticket collector came round I tried to hide in the washroom. I was hauled out, and at Waterloo I was taken for one night to Brixton prison and next morning I appeared in court. I didn't even know where I was. They sent me back to Winchester.

Time nagged by; and by the time I was eighteen I at last decided to find out who I really was. It was very simple: I sent to Stoke-on-Trent for my birth certificate. I had it sent to the address of the factory where I worked. Then came the traumatic moment of my young life, the morning when the certificate arrived. I went to the lavatory to open the fateful letter in private. It is impossible for me to put into words what I felt when I read the name of my so-called 'aunt' as my legal mother, and that of my real father as 'unknown'.

Perhaps the very worst thing about that moment was that I didn't have a single soul I could confide in. I had to walk back to the workshop and keep my secret and control my inner feelings. It was Thursday, and I said nothing at home until the following Sunday when my 'uncle' had gone out and the coast was clear. I managed to get my mother alone in the small lounge and took the birth certificate out of my pocket and handed it to her without any words. My throat was almost closed with emotion. Her face went quite hard, she never flinched; there was no compassion at all. Her only response was self-defence, although I hadn't accused her of anything. At first she said 'Your uncle isn't your father', to which I replied that I was aware of that. Then she said another strange thing 'Your father was a devil', without explaining what she meant.

73   By this time I was in such internal agony that I

rushed out of the room, and to my own little bedroom where I lay down and just wept. After that painful Sunday scene I never referred to the matter again, and pretended that it had never happened. But now I was secretly planning when I would leave Winchester and go to London. I had to wait a whole year before I got away to a new job in a factory in South London. I had been forced to buy some new clothes for the move, and also needed some money while I made the change.

I was just nineteen when I began my life-time search for happiness, but it took me three further years before I realised that I was suffering from the desperate need to love. For several years I tortured myself, quite uselessly, wondering about my father. Had he been some kind of criminal? Had I got some bad blood in me? Was he a sex maniac? Perhaps he was even a foreigner? I made no practical efforts to track him down, and the fact that I did indeed have a father like other human beings faded from my mind.

Now I was forced to live in the world. I was my own Leonardo, and had to create my own life out of nothing. I never cut myself off from the Winchester home. I simply did not have the courage or strength to be completely alone. But I've always wondered that anybody should subordinate a human life in that way to the most absurd social convention.

Jaqueline Neave

Jaqueline is thirty-one and the wife of a personnel manager earning about £4,000 a year. They have a daughter of two and a half and live in a new ranch-style house in the suburbs of Nottingham.

I did what was expected of me. It carries you over such a long time — fulfilling yourself as wife and mother, leaving school, starting work, falling in love, getting married, settling down, moving house, getting pregnant, having the baby, moving house again. I should think I've spent thirty years doing what I thought I ought to do. I never stopped to think whether it was what I wanted to do or not. And it's only now, now that Mandy's getting to be more independent that I've had time to sit down and think I've been other people's prisoner all my life. That isn't quite true, I've always been vaguely discontented, but I've been too *busy* to take any serious stand against it. I left grammar school just before A-levels because I thought I'd discovered love, and that was going to carry through the rest of my life. I was silly; but I was reasonably bright. Is that a contradiction? If I were to be brutal, I'd say 'I've put a kid in the world I'm not interested in, I'm living with a man I find utterly unintelligent, I live in a house that crushes me, I feel my life is over, my own life, and I'm not thirty.'

The happiest time in my life was being pregnant. You feel the whole world revolves around you, everybody says 'how are you?', 'would you like to sit down?' 'do take care'; then the minute the baby's born you stop being the centre of the universe and everybody's concern is transferred to baby. I think there's nobody so alone as women with young children. As they get older, five, six, it's different; you can start to treat them as companions, but until that time, it's terrifying. You panic when you're alone with your first child, you don't know what to do if anything goes wrong. I think it's different for people who stay in the same place, if you have a mother or relatives in the area, but people on this estate are nomads; they move every five minutes, husband's job, wife's aspirations to somewhere better, though why anybody should be motivated to aim for something like this only bigger and better, I shall never know. Since we've been married I've lived in four houses. Four houses in eleven years.

When I first came to Nottingham, I used to walk about with the pram for hours on end. You become grateful for the most insignificant things. If somebody smiles at you or says 'Nice day isn't it', you feel grateful. I can't tell you how alone I was then. I used to come home and cry. I couldn't talk to my husband about it. Anyway, he was having a difficult time at work; he wasn't enjoying it. He actually envied me my life; he used to come home and say wasn't I lucky pottering about here all day. Pottering. They'll potter into their graves and not notice it. He had no idea of what I was suffering. He still doesn't; he's the breadwinner, breadwinner!

We decided that I shouldn't work; so there I was in a brand-new house, with a baby, wondering what the hell I was going to do to stop myself going raving mad. And I'm still wondering, three years afterwards.

You get to know every detail of other people's lives; the arrival of the man to mend a neighbour's television is an event. I could understand any woman just taking all her clothes off and asking him in. There is a woman who lives opposite, on the other side of the Green, and I see her sitting in the window and putting make-up on. She is so careful; she spends hours there every morning. Then she comes out, immaculate, carrying a shopping bag, and two hours later she comes home, and her shopping bag is no heavier than it was when she went out. You can just tell she hasn't been anywhere special.

The only event in my day is when my husband comes home. It used to be very important to me; it was the only thing I had. But he was drained by work and never brought anything into the home, except his despair and tiredness; and all he wanted to do was be quiet and relax and not make any effort. He used to

sag visibly as he came through the front door; and my
heart sank and I thought 'Oh Christ, I'm losing my
husband as well. I can't even keep my man interested', and I used to be so tense and over-anxious
that I got on his nerves and he'd tell me to leave him
in peace or not to fuss. So I tried desperately not to
get on his nerves, and that made things worse. I've
never spoken to him about it. He doesn't know how
close we've been in the marriage to me walking out.
He knows nothing about it. At one time it used to
infuriate me, but now I feel quietly superior. I don't
want to hurt him. What I'd really like would be for
him to come home and say 'Jackie, I'm emigrating to
Australia with a girl from the typing pool.' But I
know he won't. But it needs something like that to
make me do something. Otherwise I shall probably sit
here feeling sorry for myself for the rest of my life.
Or running in and out of the other girls' houses
saying, 'Aren't men awful,' 'how's your period?'
'baby's cut a new fang'.

Mr Gibbs

Mr Gibbs is sixty-five and retired. He lives with his second wife in a council flat, four storeys up in a block on a hilltop overlooking South London. The block looks inwards to a cracked asphalt courtyard, which is enclosed on three sides by the flats, red brick, with brick balconies and fetid staircases covered with graffiti like 'Crystal Palace Mafia.'

The flat is traditionally furnished—moquette suite with cushions covered with sale remnants of material; a varnished pot-bellied sideboard, table covered with chenille cloth. On the wall there are photographs of David Cassidy, Terence Stamp and Diana Rigg, taken from colour supplements; and a wooden maple-leaf, carved with Gothic script 'The two most beautiful words I know—My Mother.'

Mr Gibbs has been a stoker, labourer, soldier and tramp; he has never remained long in one place. He has developed few ties, although he remarried three years ago, a widow from Northern Ireland.

I spent most of my young life in Tuebrook, Liverpool. We had a paper shop, and I used to sell papers in my bare feet when I was eleven. In the morning and then again at night, six till half past nine. In the war my mother drove a horse and cart for the waste-paper department. When I was eight I was sent to a convent in Blackburn. I don't know what for. I suppose I was in the way, like a lot more kids. But we weren't treated very good. I remember once having a sack over my head with circles cut out for the eyes, climbing up chimneys to clean them. I think the worst punishment was what the nuns used to do; they'd tear up your letters from home because you'd misbehaved yourself. Anyway, I ran away, and when I got home, mother took me straight to Father Berry's school — another place for naughty boys. There you had to put your clothes in a basket every night and you were locked in a dormitory. My mother didn't seem to like children at all. She was married three times in all. My father died when I was two; my mother had twenty-four children in all; my-self and my sister are the only two left. I'm the youngest. But they used to come, at certain times, from all over the world, to be with mother and father. They used to have the mucking-in spirit in them days. Then I was sent to the Royal Hibernian Military School in Dublin. My father had been an army man. I'd a step-sister in Dublin, and I was sent to stay with her. I got knocked about there, I never hardly went outside the door. But I'm no worse off for it, I can cook, clean, do the shopping, you ask the wife. Being on your own. I've written letters for thousands of people. They used to call me 'the lawyer' in the army. Blokes from the East End who couldn't write their names.

In 1922 I came to London. I had no home. I slept out, under the arches in Villiers Street, anywhere I could. I used to go round, had to make a meal of any bits and pieces out of the pig-bins. If you were picked up by the police and you were sleeping out as a youngster, they took you to Brixton Juvenile Court. 'Have you any fixed abode?' 'No.' 'Where's his parents?' 'We don't know.' 'Do his parents want him?' 'No.' Right. You were then taken in front of a magistrate, sent to Pentonville Road Home, where you got knocked from pillar to post. Chap by the name of Potts, he used to stand on your toes and hit you in the guts. You were sent to a Reformatory School — they called them Industrial Schools — where the dear Christian Brothers were so strict. If you were caught smoking, you were stood on a chair in the dining hall with a pipe full of shag in your mouth, and you smoked it till you brought your in-sides up. If you were caught stealing, you had a big night-dress on and you had a sack full of potatoes over your shoulder and you walked round and round the quad. And sometimes, if you didn't want to take part in a game, they stood you on a chair in a field, and left you there till you were nearly freezing to death. Then, when you walked down into the town with the band, all the shops shut because you were criminals. And to call a child that slept out, that had

no home, a criminal, I think it's the worst thing anybody could've done. That's what happened to me.

I've slept out all over London. We used to go and
pick up vegetables at Covent Garden. We used to wait
for the Silver Lady of a night to come in her caravan.
We used to get cigarettes, tea, bread and marge. We
went down to Webber Street to the soup kitchen
there; you got a chitty given you there for a bowl of
soup and bread; if you wanted to make an extra
couple of bob any time, you could go round to the
boxing ring at Blackfriars, and put the gloves on with
some of the boxers. I had my ear closed and a broken
nose, but you got paid for it.

I used to go to the Church Army, and you'd get a
night's bed, bread and soup, and you chopped up
wood in the morning, and then you weren't allowed
back there for a month. I slept on top of the Underground at Charing Cross because it was nice and
warm there. There was a place called the Metro-
politan Asylum Board, where you reported if you
came from out of London and if you were decently
dressed, they sent you to the Church Army, and if
you weren't, you got a domino to travel on the tram
to the workhouse at Lambeth. Some nights we'd sit
in the crypt of St Martin's, sit bolt upright all night
long; next morning you'd be turned out, not a bite of
food, not even a wash.

Eventually I walked from London to Liverpool and
got a job helping the recruiting officer up there. I
joined the 12th Lancers at Canterbury in 1925, I was
in the army eleven years. I got married in 1937, when
I was thirty-one; and I worked as a stoker at Rowton
House, Newington Butts. I joined the Fire Service in
1939. We were bombed out four times. I had my
chest badly damaged. In 1956 my wife died, I was
left with a boy of twelve and a girl of six. We lived in
furnished rooms all over. I was in and out of hospitals. I had a furnished room at Euston till 1968 when
the Kennedy Hotel was built. My landlady was sent
to Dunstable and I was offered a place in an old per-
sons' home, at the age of sixty-one. I got married in
1969; and now here we are, up four flights of stairs,

at the top of a hill, sixty steps to climb everytime we go out.

The workhouses were terrible places. I know all the spikes from London to Liverpool. At Newark, you slept on a stone floor, and in the middle there was a piss-bucket. There was forty blokes, half of them would come in half soaked with drink, and it was pitch black; sometimes in the morning you'd be swimming in it. Then next morning, you'd get your six ounces of bread and your two ounces of cheese. When you went in the workhouse, you took off every stitch of clothing, you put all your property in your hat, you had a bath, your clothes were cleaned. You got nothing for nothing. All the shops knew who you were, and if anything went missing, you had the police after you five minutes later. If you knocked on a door, begging 'Can I have something to eat?' they'd say 'Wait there a minute'; then nip round the back and call a copper. I've slept on barges in Hull, in a cemetery, in empty trains.

When I was on the road, you'd go to a farm and say 'Look, if there's anything you want doing and you're willing to give me a meal and a place to sleep,' he might say 'Well, you can sleep over the black-smith's shop or sleep in a cowshed', and you'd give a hand and get a few bob. I went pea-picking, I could always earn a few bob doing farm-work, or in a butcher's shop, scrubbing the block down. There's no need for anybody to be idle. In 1937, there was no work so two of us got a pot of black paint and went round painting railings and shoe-scrapers and door-knobs, and in two days we'd earned ourselves four pounds. There's no need for anybody at present not to have work. You can go cleaning windows, clearing gardens, trimming hedges. You can always get work, only they don't do it.

In them days, it wasn't your fault if you didn't have a home. In 1928 when I was working on Unilever House I got the sack for dropping a basket of tiles from a plank, sixty feet up. I nearly fell, it was either the tiles or me. And I was living with my brother-in-law at the time, and when I got home, he nearly killed me. And I was twenty-one then. I can honestly say I've never had a real home of my own. As a kid, it wasn't your home. When we lived in Liverpool, the front room was mother's; nobody was allowed to sit in there but mother. When she called you to sit at the table, you sat at the table, and when you'd finished you stood up and said 'Thank God for my good dinner', whatever you'd eaten, 'please mother may I leave the table', and you had to get permission before you could go. Before you went to school, the girls made the beds and the boys cleaned the grate or any other work.

When I was in the army my money was ten shillings a week, and out of that you had to buy blacking and dubbin; you had to buy polish, Brasso — all your cleaning stuff. Then they'd charge you two shillings for the regimental history book, one and six for a walking out cane, a shilling for a drink-ing mug and six and six for gym kit. And a lot of people didn't know, but when you were in India you were even paying towards your coffin, 'cos a lot of them died. A lot of them had malaria. You had no rights at all.

I was thirty-one when I got married. I'd never had a woman before. She was all right at first, but she took to drink and some nights I wouldn't see her at all, she'd be out all night. She worked in the toilets up at the Zoo, and there was a lot of Irishwomen worked there, and on their way home they'd stop in every pub for a drink. It killed her in the end. Liver. It does you no good. I've two children. I did my best for them. They don't seem to want to know you.

I went back to Liverpool last year. It's changed. No kids in the streets. We were always in the street, and on a Saturday morning we packed a case with bread and dripping and some lemonade and we went up the park and stopped there and enjoyed ourselves. We were quite happy. We hadn't much to eat, it was more of the mucking-in spirit though. When I went back nobody wanted to talk to you, nobody was interested. I think this progress that everybody talks about, it might be all right for some, but to take an

82

old person out of a house where they've lived for
years, and put them in any flat, and then try to tell
them they're happy — they're not. They've lost their
neighbours, they've lost their friends. We never used
to have the trouble we have now. You got one round
the ear from a policeman or you got sent to your
home and they dealt with you. But the policeman
was law then, and you respected your parents. Your
mother was your mother and your father was your
father, there was no such thing as walking out, leaving
home for the least little thing. And we looked after
our parents, we respected them. They were strict,
terrible strict. My sister was twenty-two, and she was
courting, and she had to be in by six o'clock in
winter, nine o'clock in summer. That's how strict it
was. Same at school. If you stepped out of line you
got the cane. But it done us no harm. They say we
musn't punish them. Well, what are we to do? Let
people be mugged and have their houses smashed?

My sister was more of a mother to me, the sister
who's dead now. She was the only one who took care
of me. One day my mother took me to the dentist, to
have some teeth out. When we came out she said 'I'm
going home now on the tram, you find your own way
home.' When I came home, my mouth was all
bleeding, and my sister washed it out and all that, and
laid me down on the couch, and when my mother
came home she nearly killed me because I hadn't
been to school in the afternoon. That's what my
mother was. She wanted a high life. She's been a
matron in the Indian hospitals. She'd been reading to
a blind Parsee, getting money when she was abroad.
She didn't want the family. When she was in India,
my sister Maggie died in a convent in Dublin. They
sent a telegram to my mother, asking her what to do,
and she just said 'Bury her'. That's all the interest she
had in the children. Once you came to the age of
reason, school, out. There she is, that's my mother.
[*A sepia oval photograph of a woman with an abundant
chignon, a large and gently undulating breast, one
hand on an occasional table, the other holding an
ostrich feather.*] She loved nice clothes, she loved

dancing. When she was matron in India, my father was a guard on Lord Kitchener's train, and they had plenty of money, you see, she was having a high life. Then she found she'd got to come down, and she didn't like it. The children suffered. Life's like making a cup of tea — it's how you make it. My father was 6 foot 4½ inches tall, he was forty-eight chest, took a 22½" collar. He was a sergeant saddler in the Artillery, and he could drink like a fish. He was a marvellous man, cheerful. He was a lot better than my mother. I really believe he died of a broken heart through her going out night after night, same as my first wife did.

I don't belong to any party or any religion. I call myself a Christian. I believe in this: if you see a man down, try and pick him up. If you can't pick him up, don't kick him down any further, leave him where he is. I've always had a motto in my life, that was over my bed years ago: 'I worried about having no shoes, till I met a man with no feet.' I've always got on through trying to be cheerful and helping others. I've been very lonely. I don't make friends easily. I don't like a crowd.

Mrs Grafton

Mrs Grafton is in her early fifties and lives in a comfortable neo-Georgian house in the home counties. She is soft-spoken and subdued and ascribes her apparent calm to the effect of drugs she has been receiving after a stay in a psychiatric hospital. Her husband is an executive with a cosmetics firm in Portsmouth and she has three children, the oldest of whom is now twenty.

He's married; a bit of a drop-out I suppose you could call him; very independent. He left school and went to work in a subnormality hospital. Nobody was more surprised than I was. It did him a lot of good. He's now starting at university: politics, economics. My second son has been working as a laboratory technician since he left school; and I've a daughter who's still at school.

People say to me sometimes 'I can't understand it, why should you be ill, depression, you've a good husband, three attractive children, you've a reasonable income.' It's as though you only had a right to psychiatric illness if you can prove that the outward circumstances justify it. People only look at externals, as though the cause of depression or anxiety could be found there. Of course, it's inside you, it's part of you. It's chemical — perhaps it needs something to activate it, I don't know. I've always been rather sensitive. I've never found it easy to relate to other people. It goes back to my childhood, I suppose. I was an only child — so is my husband incidentally. It means that we've had no one we can really turn to. You feel the lack of a family at times like these. The neighbours have been very good, but you don't feel you can make demands on them in the same way that you can on those tied to you by blood.

I suppose the very fact that I was an only child indicates that there was something wrong with my parents' marriage. We lived in Highgate, and we were comfortably off. My father was an importer. We suffered a little in the depression. We moved to a block of flats that seemed ultra-modern then. They look dreadful now, don't they. My parents were sexually incompatible. I was aware that things were not right between them. One day, when I was about fifteen, my mother took me on her knee — can you imagine such a thing? My daughter would think i was mad if I tried to take her on my knee, and she's much younger than I was then — but I accepted it, and she told me that my father didn't love her any more, and that he had another woman instead. He had a girl-friend, a redhead like my mother, and my mother got to hear of it. I was absolutely shattered. I didn't know how to react. I'd always got on better with my father than my mother. I was horrified beyond words.

I used to go to my friends' houses, and their families had always seemed so much happier than mine. I used to go home and weep, oh not once, but night after night. But that one incident really had a most damaging effect upon me. I really do think sometimes that if I hadn't been subjected to that, things might have been different. I loathed my mother. I didn't realise it until years later. Everybody thought I was devoted to her. We used to go out to-gether, to theatres, museums, concerts, and the fact that we had the same interests obscured the real truth, that fundamentally I hated her. When we used to go to the theatre, she had a very loud voice, and she always made a commotion wherever she went. She was always a source of turbulence and noise. They used to have trays of tea in the intervals at the theatre in those days, and hers always rattled the loudest. I was always embarrassed. I didn't know what I really felt, I used to go all hot under the collar and wish I was a million miles away. It isn't until later that things, feelings crystallise. She was so domina-ting. When you're young, you just accept, you don't question what is there. Of course I hated my father when she told me that he didn't love her any more. I thought he must have been wicked; I resented him furiously. It was only later I realised that she'd tried to involve me in her warfare against him. She was, I suppose, afraid of being alone herself. A lot of the things people inflict upon each other come from a fear of being alone.

I was twenty-seven before I left home. In fact, I did that through illness. There would have been no other way that I could see of getting free from her influence. I had a breakdown then, and I now realise — I didn't know then of course — that it was my way of asserting my freedom, and escaping from a hateful situation. But I was younger then, I was more resilient, I recovered completely then.

Only now, after this time, my recovery seems so fragile, so precarious. I feel I'm on the edge of an abyss that could open up again at any moment. There's a cycle of depression, and then of stability, and I'm not in control of it. It's very frightening. This very fact that it doesn't correspond to outward circumstances is frightening. Being mentally ill is an experience you can't describe to anyone. You're quite alone with it. Even those you love and who love you are quite powerless to do anything for you.

I spent several months in hospital. Fortunately, I was in a psychiatric ward in a general hospital, which I think is a good idea. It goes a long way to remove the stigma of mental illness. I had psychotherapy, electrotherapy, drugs — I was sent home only two days after the electrotherapy. Then another kind of loneliness began. Of all the treatment I had, I think the most helpful was psychotherapy, being able to talk about things. I was told I had a personality disorder. It's funny, a long time afterwards I've thought of things I might have said to the psychiatrist but by then it's too late. You're at a disadvantage. They say things to you which you accept as true at the time, and then you wonder afterwards what on earth he meant by them. One ought to be able to have the opportunity to come back at them, ask them to explain themselves.

The illness took a long time to creep up on me. I felt myself breaking down gradually. You can't describe the feeling. Concentration goes, you wander about, not quite knowing what you're doing. I used to sit down, try to write out a shopping list, and I'd write 'baked beans' and then my mind would go blank and I'd just sit there. Fortunately the children were there and that helped me to cope for a while. You're filled with oppression, dread, anxiety that something terrible is going to happen all the while. You're afraid of the outside world, of people, you feel they're a threat to you; whereas of course what is really happening is not outside at all, but inside you. It culminated when my husband went on a business trip to Japan. He went away for a month. I got quite desperate. I didn't dare go out. Everything outside the front door seemed hostile, noisy, big. Even to go for a walk, to go shopping was an impossible undertaking. I used to lie in bed, perhaps till mid-day, and then get up and wander around, or just sit there. I couldn't eat. I lost two stone during that month. I couldn't even write to my husband, I didn't have the will to. Anyway, it was during the postal strike, so even if I'd been able to, he wouldn't have got it. Then one day, they rang up from his firm, from Portsmouth, and said they were sorry, but he'd be three days later coming home than they'd anticipated. I suppose I broke down then, I started crying, 'Send him home, please send him home, why can't he come home.' They evidently realised I was ill, and they sent a first aid nurse round from the firm. She was very nice, but it wasn't at all what I needed.

When my husband came home, he was appalled to see the state I was in. He sent for the doctor at once, and I was taken to hospital. I knew a frightful loneliness there, too. And of course, my husband was under stress too, he had no one he could talk to about all that was happening. I expect he felt guilty too, although of course it wasn't his fault.

After being in hospital seven months, I was discharged very unceremoniously. The PSW said 'If you want any further help, contact the Social Services Department.' Well I'd had no experience of the Social Services, I didn't know what was available and what wasn't. We'd never asked for anything or ever had any need of them. My husband was very angry. He said 'Isn't there someone you could put us in touch with?' They left us to make shift for ourselves, and of course we did nothing. My own doctor got me a home help. Then one day, in a bookshop, I saw a Penguin book about the Social Services, and that's the way I found out about the statutory services and the available help. So I asked our GP if he would arrange for a Psychiatric Social Worker from the local authority to come and see me, which he did. She was very good, and helped me a great deal. She came once a fort-night. But I thought it was disgraceful that I should learn of what services are available through a paper-back book I happened to pick up by chance. There ought to have been some follow-up from the hospital.

The neighbours were very kind. Some of them used to cook things and bring them in to me. But you can't help noticing people's reactions, the stigma that mental illness still has. Some of them think that an antidote to depression is in being bright all the time, and avoid mentioning things they think might upset you, whereas the more you can talk about it, the better it is. Then there are others who obviously don't mention it at all, but it's there in their minds all the time; they're always slightly nervous, as though you might suddenly do something desperate. There was a lady, very well-intentioned but not very sensi-tive, who said to me 'Well you know you're always welcome to call, if you feel you need to.' How could you call if somebody says that to you? Any visit, a casual knock on the door, she'd think straight away that you were in dire need, and they'd be terrified. The best way is to be treated quite naturally, and this is something people find hard to understand.

I still feel that my recovery is incomplete. I can't quite trust myself. I would do something, meals on wheels or something like that, but I'm afraid of this gulf of depression. If it comes, I know I shall let everybody down. I've never felt the need of a career, being a wife and mother when the children were small was always quite enough. I used to love the piano, but I don't play now. I like writing. I wrote a poem when I felt I couldn't communicate to anybody the feeling of my depression.

Lost time drifting away
Closed in the depths of the mind
Sadness nearing madness
Loneliness of the soul past bearing.

Living in isolation among people and doing
Dreading each day — longing for sleep,
Separation from family — dead to all feeling.

Trapped in a cage, powerless to move,
Thought dulled but sickening.
Where is the answer — where the release?

Death could be one way — hope must remain
Somewhere a key must be found
To unlock the secret that makes life worth living.

Mrs Wyman

Mrs Wyman is forty-eight and left her husband just over a year ago. She works as a secretary and rents a flat in a large Edwardian villa. Her younger son shares the flat and her elder son has a bed-sitting room in the same house.

My husband is Scottish. He was very ambitious. He had a poor background, and started work after the war as a bus-conductor. But he was terribly ambitious, and he worked his way up to become traffic manager. He was completely ruthless. Very determined; hard-working, he has some very good qualities. He has only two weaknesses. One is that I don't believe he has ever performed a kind action in his life; and the other is that he is very incompetent as a lover. A man should pleasure a woman, shouldn't he? Well my husband never succeeded. In a way, that's why he turned against me. I'm the only person who knows how vulnerable he is. With everybody else he's hard, ruthless.

But he always would have his own way. I began to lose my identity with him. He was destroying my personality. You don't notice it. It happens little by little over the years, and you think things are still the same, nothing's changed. But it has. You fool yourself, you deliberately blind yourself, but the time comes when you have to take action, unless you want to disintegrate completely. In a way, the self-assertion all the time perhaps comes from the inadequacies. The desire for power over people can be caused by realising your weaknesses, and trying to cover them up.

I hadn't left him a fortnight before his woman moved in with him. I loved him so much; it's terrible to love someone that much. You'll go on for years and years, making allowances, deluding yourself that everything's all right. He only wanted to take, take, take. It's unbelievable, the cruelty I suffered. When you're out of it, you can hardly believe you've been through such incredible experiences, but while you're living them, it seems natural in a way, part of the nightmare. He used to hide things, a vase, a dish, a piece of furniture, and then swear I'd done it. He'd come in in the evenings, and look round for something that wasn't in its place, to find fault with. He convinced me I was a mental case. I went to the doctor, and I saw a psychiatrist, and when I'd finished talking to him he said 'I think it's probably your husband who is sick.' It went on for years. He used to tell me things and then deny he'd said them, or swear he'd said things he hadn't even mentioned. I thought I was going mad. I began to doubt the evidence of my own senses. It's a frightening experience, I used to panic sometimes. But I never lost my temper with him. I'd always keep quite calm, but of course he hated that more than anything. He'd get furious and storm out of the house. But as soon as he'd gone, I'd break down, I'd be all trembling. I used to ring the Samaritans. I don't know what I'd have done without the man who was my counsellor. He really helped me to understand and be able to fight back, otherwise I really do think I would have gone mad. I was a victim of a campaign of persecution. I never told any family or friends about it. I couldn't imagine that he could be doing all the things he did as a premeditated plan. But now it's all over I can see that it was part of an attempt to drive me away.

It was a difficult decision for me; to decide to leave, at my time of life, after you've been with somebody for over twenty years. I used to sit in this flat at first, and listen for every car that stopped nearby. And I'd think 'That's Ken', then of course I'd remember and say to myself 'Don't be stupid, it can't be.' Sometimes I've wondered who on earth there is to turn to. My parents are dead, and the one person I thought loved me turns out like this. It was all one side, all these years. The love was all on my side. I've got the boys, they've done quite well. They're interested in cars, engineering, mechanical things. I try to take an interest. Sometimes I have this dread, suppose they turn out the same as their father. You can't help wondering. My only hope is that they'll get married, and I shall be able to be friends with their wives. What other chance have I got for meeting people? It's so difficult to start again, when you thought you were secure for life. I haven't been able to afford to go out anywhere. My youngest boy is still at college, I haven't even mentioned the financial aspect of things. As if one didn't have enough to put up with without all the worry of how to get from day to day. I don't know, perhaps it's the trivial things that turn out to be your salvation in the end. They can take your mind off the basic problems.

There are so many places a woman can't go to on her own. All the people I know now are women, how could I meet anyone else? There simply isn't the opportunity. I write poetry, I write all the time. It comes quite naturally. That does help me, I must admit; it keeps me sane. I've always had this urge to write. I could never have talked to Ken about it. He believed in keeping women in their place. Being a Scot — I think in the north they don't consider the woman except as someone to keep the house in order and to go to bed with. I think that's one of the reasons why he resents me so, because he knows he never really satisfied me. That's why people get so aggressive sometimes. It's quite true that it all goes back to sex. I knew very little when I got married, and I do know friends of mine who knew nothing at all, and had to be told the facts of life on their wedding night by their husband. It can be a dreadful experience. The youngsters know a lot more these days. It's a good thing. A woman should know what she's getting when she gets married. It shouldn't come as a shock to her. I think perhaps it's gone to the other extreme now, they overdo it a bit. On the television, you see women being kissed in a way — I've never been kissed like that. Perhaps I've missed something. It's funny how you notice that all the TV adverts, everything is geared towards couples, to marriage. Everything you see sort of reminds you of the fact that you're alone, that you don't have anybody.

I've seen my whole life suddenly become insecure.

You realise that you've got to provide for your own future and retirement, you're completely on your own. After twenty years I walked out on him. I didn't even have the boys with me. They stayed with him at first. They must have thought I was in the wrong. It wasn't until he moved his woman in with him that they began to realise. That was too much for them, and they asked if they could come and move in with me.

I had to do it though. It got so that I even began to doubt that I existed. Of course, there are always two sides to a story. I expect if you heard his version it would be quite different. But nothing can disguise the fact that for all those years I was the one to give in. He almost annihilated me. I don't think any girl getting married today would stand for that kind of treatment.

I do believe in God, that's been a help to me. I've been reading this book, do you know it? *Bring out the Magic in your Mind* by Al Koran. He says that if you think about something all the time, you can get it, by concentrating on it. You work towards it sub-consciously all the time. I believe in positive thinking. It's will-power. You could just let yourself go like some people do. You have to say to yourself 'I can, I will, I must.'

[*Mrs Wyman is a quiet, rather subdued woman; smart, with silver-blue hair, a low voice with a slight London accent. She wears a perplexed and anxious look, and plays constantly with the row of pearls over her pale blue sweater. With the copy of the* Magic in Your Mind *was a copy of* The Chariot of the Gods.]

I've tried joining clubs. It isn't difficult to have a full life, in the sense of occupied. But no amount of social life can compensate for the lack of something in your existence, some meaning. On the other hand, it isn't true to say it's worth putting up with anything for the sake of company. It isn't. It is better to be alone and have your self-respect and peace of mind than be with someone and subjected to humiliation and insults every minute of the day. At least I'm now at peace. He put me out of the house in the end. I had nowhere to go. He had no kindness in him at all. But all the same, whatever he's done to me, I miss him. I miss him terribly.

Con Stoddart

Con Stoddart works in a tannery. He is fifty-three and has a wife and two children. He owns a small terraced house. He is a small, shabby man whose appearance contrasts oddly with his anarchic and vitriolic social attitudes. He wears a yellowing silk muffler and rides a bicycle. He was brought up in great poverty and in the tradition of independent, disaffected shoemakers. He speaks in a monotone which tends, at first, to obscure the nature of his discourse.

Lonely, I'm bloody lonely, and so's every other poor sod that works in a factory. Forced labour, that's what I am. I had no choice. They didn't give me any skills, they didn't train me for anything. I'll tell you what my education did for me. It trained me to shovel shit; and then they turned round and said 'What can you do?' I said 'Well I can shovel shit.' So they said 'Is that all you can do? That's all you're fit for then.' It was 1933 when I left school. Golden year in the history of human civilisation that was. Six kids in the family — my old man had been out of work two years. I got a job as delivery boy for a butcher. Deliver a bullet straight into his fat gut, the old bastard. I had a bike I could hardly reach the pedals, sit up and beg. Story of my life that is. It had a carrier at the front, and I carried trays of meat covered with a white cloth. I wore a straw hat and a white apron, and I knocked on doors where domestic servants came out with silver trays, and sometimes the missis used to come and wag her fat finger at me and say 'Yesterday's chop wasn't fresh.' I did that for three years, till I asked for more money and they sacked me because they could get some other poor mutt just from school to do it cheaper.

I've got up at six o' clock every morning of my working life. My body isn't allowed the sleep it needs. I'm woken by an alarm clock, Westclox. They made a fortune out of waking up the working man, until an invention was made that put him back to sleep again.

Do you know what that is? Television they call it. I eat at twelve o' clock, not because I'm hungry but because that's when the hooter goes. I go home at half past five, crawl back into bed and set the alarm for the next morning. I can smoke forty fags a day. HM Government puts on the packet 'Smoking Can Damage Your Health,' not 'Cigarettes Kill You Quicker,' because they don't want to give up their revenue, and throw thousands of poor sods out of work who've been trained to pack cigarettes instead of reaching for the stars. I can fill me gut with beer that tastes better when it's been through your bloody bladder. And now I can watch television. Have you ever watched it? No I mean it, seriously, really watched it? Really looked. They never take more than one sip of a double brandy, they live in apartments like the 'Queen Elizabeth', and every five minutes they break off so some fat overpaid pouf can go into ecstasies about some chemical garbage that's a revolution in dehydrated corn-flakes. I'm already a walking robot, but that's still not good enough — they can get an even better machine to replace me, and they'll like that better. And do you know why? Because machines can't vote, can't go on the club or the dole, don't eat. But there's one big flaw, machines can't spend money either, so how are they going to make their profit. You can only squeeze profit out of people; machines can't buy their junk and line their bloody pockets.

What's my life? Two weeks holiday, horsemeat and lettuce leaves and two nights' kip on the floor at Luton airport. Bank Holiday, go and gawp at the treasures the rich piled up on the backs of my ancestors. Marriage. Expect you to put it in the same place forty years, I get more of a kick out of taking me socks off. Kids, they turn round 'My friend Sheila's got a room of her own to study in. Why can't I have one?' Then the Council comes and tells you they want your house for a motorway. Not to grow wheat for the starving millions, not for shelter for the homeless, but to speed everybody on their way to the casualty wards. They come and ask

97

you if you can make alternative arrangements for accommodation. I bring home sixteen quid a week, I said 'Yes, we'll move in with you.' The missis works on the Twilight Shift. She lives on the twilight shift. We all do. She says I'm not normal. We all want to better ourselves; there's only one way we'll be better and that's when we've got buttercups growing out of our arseholes.

The trouble with me, I'm different. I see everybody else, them I work with, family, everybody, suck up the swill that's being chucked at them, bettering themselves, pinching and scraping and worrying themselves silly about where the next — not square meal, mind you, but where the next new car is coming from. You hear them, my missis squawking about her ambitions. Ambitions. It all revolves round wall to wall carpets. Ambition. You know what my trouble is? I'm a nihilist. I'm fifty-three. They tell me I've had the best years of my life, and they were fucking terrible. All I'm doing now is filling in time till I croak. All them at work, they're talking about their retirement as if they were going to be re-born. Half of 'em won't reach it, and the other half'll lay on their backs staring into space, while their kids pray to God the money'll come to them in time for a trip to the Costa Brava.

There might be life after death, I couldn't care less, there's sod-all before it, that's all I know.

Mrs Nichols

Mrs Nichols is in her mid-forties, divorced and childless. She has been very ill and lives off Social Security. She dresses smartly and when I met her was wearing a tweed costume, diamanté earrings, engagement and wedding rings. She has fair hair, lacquered immaculately into stiff curls. She chain smokes, and carries an Oriental-design leather handbag, held together by an elastic band. Her gestures are nervous, and have a function other than reinforcement of her speech. She searches her handbag constantly, for cigarettes, matches, handkerchief. As she talks, she becomes very emotional, and cries from time to time. It is she, however, who insists that she will continue.

I've been so lonely I could write a book about it. I'm the one who ought to be writing the book.

I didn't have a very happy childhood. My parents were separated, and we were brought up on a council estate in Leicester. I got married as soon as I could. I know what you think I'm going to say — I was too young, I didn't know my own mind. But you're wrong; it wasn't a mistake. For seven years I was really happy. That's all I've got now, the memory of those years.

Lorrie, my husband, was a displaced person, Lithuanian. That wasn't his real name, but that's what I called him. I didn't know much about him when I married him. But that didn't matter. We were happy. Then after a few years, things started to go wrong.

He'd been out for a drink with a friend of his one Sunday dinner-time. I was waiting on the doorstep for him, chatting to some of the women over the road. They were on his mate's motorbike. The motorbike pulled up sharply and the driver's head jerked back and hit Lorrie on the forehead. He was wearing a crash helmet, but Lorrie wasn't. And he complained of a headache all that day, and that night, when we went to bed, he started to have an epileptic fit. I was scared, because I'd never seen one before, but I'd heard that they can choke, they can swallow their tongue. So I sent for the doctor, and he didn't seem worried. He said it would soon pass. It did; but he started to have them regular. Anyway, from that day, you can believe it or not, but his whole personality changed. He'd been kind and considerate, couldn't do enough for me. But now he became really quarrelsome, and of course, he started drinking. It was terrible. I know alcoholism's a disease, I know you should have sympathy with them, but he got so violent, he used to knock me about. I used to sit at home, dreading him coming in, and I used to sit there, all of a tremble, wondering what he'd do to me. Sometimes he didn't come home all night long, but it was more than I dared to ask him where he'd been. When he was drunk, he was a different person. I hardly recognised him. But afterwards, he used to cry and say 'Don't leave me Joyce.' It was heartbreaking. When he had the drink in him, he wasn't human, but afterwards, he was like a child. He used to say 'I can't help it', and of course, I used to put up with it. Once when he was drunk, he said a funny thing to me, he said 'When I was a child, they used to put me in a straightjacket.' And he'd never talked about his childhood before. If I'd ever mentioned it, he'd say no, he didn't want to remember it. Whether he'd had some sort of mental illness I don't know. When he was sober, I asked him, I said 'What did you mean about being put in a straightjacket?' He denied that he'd ever said any such thing. Anyway, he used to be away from home for days on end, I couldn't sit there and wait for him to come home, I was only in my twenties. I thought, well I've a right to live as well as him.

Anyway, I met another chap, an American. Lorrie came home less and less and I got very friendly with him. His name was Gray, and in the end, he asked me to go away with him. His own marriage was breaking up at that time and his wife and kid were going back to the States, so he was on his own. He was a serviceman, at one of the bases, and they used to come into town on Saturday night, and that's how I met him. I thought, Well I'm not breaking up his marriage, because it's already broken, like mine. Lorrie had been away for three months. I hadn't seen or heard a sound from him — he might as well have been dead. So I agreed to go away with Gray. I got all ready, I packed. I thought I'd start a new life. The night before I went away he came back. Why he should have chosen that night, I shall never know. I wondered since if it was a sign to me, not to go away. He was in a terrible state. He looked neglected and pathetic. He pleaded with me not to leave him. He said he'd stop drinking and make a new start. I'd heard it all before though. He clung to me, and begged me to stay, and said he'd got nobody in the world but me.

But I went. We got the train to Stoke-on-Trent. God knows why. I think it was easy to rent houses there cheap. That was on the Saturday. By the next Wednesday I knew I'd made a mistake. Gray wasn't everything he appeared to be. I wrote to Lorrie telling him that I'd made a mistake, and asking whether I should come back, but for some reason I never posted it. I wonder if I'd posted it I might have saved him. I just left it. And then the next day, they came, the police came to tell me he'd committed suicide.

Gray drove me back to Leicester. I was sobbing and crying all the way. I couldn't believe it. Gray was very good, he helped me through it. I had to go and identify the body, and make arrangements for the funeral. All the time I was thinking why didn't I post that letter.

At the funeral there was a lot of his Lithuanian friends. There were a lot here at that time — they'd come over from Russia — and a crowd of them turned up for the funeral. But the awful thing was a woman came out of the crowd, and in front of all the mourners she came up to me and abused me at the top of her voice. She called me everything from a pig to a dog. As if it wasn't bad enough already. I discovered afterwards it was Gray's mother-in-law. It made me so ashamed. And from that day I started to feel this terrible guilt. I felt I'd killed Lorrie. I could have prevented it. I say to myself If only, if, if, if...

So many things. I don't know. I believe that what is to be will be, I don't know. Could I have prevented him from doing it? I've lived with this feeling of guilt and reproach. I know I contributed to it. It's something you can't get rid of. Other people tell you not to worry about it; they don't blame you. But you blame yourself, and that's worse.

We went back to Stoke, and stayed there for twelve months. All during that time we made a lot of friends, and I was the life and soul of the party. But nobody knows what goes on inside of you. At times, I could have screamed with the loneliness of it, this feeling of remorse. And nobody knew, not even Gray. After a time, he said 'Why don't we go to the States, make a new start?' I jumped at it. I thought if I could get away from England, everything might be all right. We went to his home. It was a town a bit smaller than Leicester, in Virginia.

I'd lived with my first husband fourteen years, and I was with Gray four. He'd saved up a bit of money, so we were able to buy a small house. But I hated it. I hated America. The first thing that happened when we moved into the new house, he gave me a gun and said 'Don't ever on any account answer the doorbell without the gun in your hand.' A gun, it was like an extra hand to them. Whatever else I'd had to put up with, I'd never come across anything quite like this. All the housewives had guns in their handbags, and they slept with them under the pillow. Anyway, you get to accept that. But soon afterwards I became ill. I had a hysterectomy, and then they found I'd got cervical cancer, and I very nearly died. On top of all this I had a cholecystectomy. I was in hospital seven months, I had a tube in my side. For weeks I was at death's door. And of course, over there you have to pay for everything. And during the time I was so ill my husband abandoned me.

When I was just beginning to convalesce, I remember, he came in one day, and I noticed he'd got a new suit on, new shoes, a whole new outfit. And he wheeled me in my chair down the corridor to the front door, and outside there was a new blue Pontiac.

And I said 'Where did that come from?' and he said 'I bought it'. But we'd got a joint account, and this meant he couldn't spend money without my consent. So I asked him, and he said 'But you signed'. And I remembered one day he'd come in, and I had this vague memory that he'd guided my hand while I signed a piece of paper. I was too ill or drugged to know what was happening. And I'd given him the right to do what he liked with all our money. He'd spent every penny. Of course, I didn't find that out at first. After a time they said at the hospital that they could do no more for me, and they were sending me home.

Gray was away most of the time. They sent me home, and sent a nurse in to look after me. I realised by then that things were all wrong between us. I don't know how I kept my sanity. Yes, I do know. There was a neighbour who had a little girl of ten, and she used to come and sit with me and talk to me, and I honestly believe if it hadn't been for that little girl, I wouldn't be here now. But one day she said to her mother 'Mommy, shall I tell Joyce that I saw Gray with a lady?' And then of course I knew, although I'd guessed already that he'd got someone else.

And then he disappeared. Just took off and went. And I was left with a bill for eight thousand dollars for all the medical treatment, doctors' fees, hospital, dressings, everything. At that time I weighed four and a half stone.

It was horrible. While I was at death's door I must have been visited by hundreds of — they don't call them vicars — ministers, priests, clergymen. They used to come into the wards and look in the chief nurse's office at the list of all those who were critically ill, and come and pray with them. And they said things like 'I understand you don't have long to live, shall we pray together?' But as for real help, I got nothing except from that little girl. They could have prayed for eight thousand dollars.

When Gray had gone, I tried to commit suicide. But don't let anybody tell you suicide is the coward's way out, it's the hardest thing in the world. I had these tablets from the doctor, and I was in bed, and I said to the little girl one night 'Pass me my tablets' and she said 'Momma said you're only to have two' and I said 'I want all of them'; and she gave them to me, and I poured them all out on to a tray in front of me, and I looked at them, and honestly, I wanted to take them, I wanted to die. But I could not. I didn't dare. And I didn't. But I believe that I must have been spared for some purpose, only I don't know what that purpose is. I wonder if Gray going and leaving me was a punishment for what I'd done to Lorrie. You don't know, do you? You never know.

I was completely alone. I had to go on welfare, and you've no idea what a humiliation that can be. I had to sell the house, I had to sell everything I had before they'd give me a penny. And then I got seventy-five dollars a month. Once a fortnight I had to go and stand in the queue for the welfare handout, with junkies, blacks — not that I'm prejudiced, I'm not, I'm just telling you — Chinese, alcoholics, all sorts, and then I was given a seven pound bag of lentils, seven pounds of rice, some sugar and some bread. I had to go to the welfare board, and the questions they asked me! It was worse than the old Board of Guardians ever knew how to be, and I'd never been used to anything like that. Although we were only an ordinary working-class family, we'd always been independent. And of course, I couldn't begin to pay the hospital bill. They tried to trace my husband, but he'd left the state. And if anybody really wants to disappear in America, they can. I'd no one to turn to. The doctor who'd done my operation was good to me. He was a Filippino, and he told me to write to my relatives in England, or if I didn't he would, and tell them what was happening. So I wrote to my brother, and I got a letter back straight away, saying he was coming over to collect me. But he was only an ordinary working-class chap, living in a council house, I wrote back and said I'd scrape the fare together and come home. But before I could leave the country, the medical authorities made my brothers sign to say that they would guarantee that I would pay back the eight thousand dollars I owed.

The doctor was very good. He arranged for a wheel-chair at the airport, and saw to it that I was looked after on the flight home. And when I got to Heathrow, my two brothers were there to meet me. They didn't recognise me. I weighed four and a half stone, I was a bag of walking bones. We were all sobbing our hearts out, I felt dreadful. Anyway, one of them took me in a car to his house, and they'd cleared the children out of the back bedroom, and of course I was very ill, I didn't even know where I was. I lay there for weeks with the curtains drawn, I couldn't take an interest in anything. Then one morning, I felt a bit better, the sun was streaming through the curtains, so I got up to go to the window and look at the view; and his house was overlooking the cemetery, the very spot where my first husband was buried.

I stayed there for some months, and gradually, I got a bit stronger. But one of the neighbours had done a bit of snooping, and reported to the council that I was living there. Somebody came from the council and told him that I had a week to get out or my brother and his family would be evicted. I don't think they can do that actually, but my brother was scared — he's got five children. So there I was, hardly able to walk, looking for somewhere to stay. Eventually, I moved in with a friend of mine, who had just got remarried, but she lives in a council house as well, and the same thing has happened there. I told the Social Security I was paying her four pounds a week rent, which I am, and so they've been allowing me £9.40 a week, which is supposed to include not only rent, but a high protein diet as well, believe it or not. But she denied it to the council, that I was paying her anything at all, and so I've got to get out of there now. I did find a flat, but the rent was £7.50 a week, and Social Security said they wouldn't pay that much rent. So I'm still looking for somewhere. I've been to see bed-sitters, but they're dirty and dingy. I'm still a sick woman. I don't know what I shall do.

Mrs Maycock

Mrs Maycock is seventy-four and a widow. She lives off her pension in a small terraced cottage in a country town. The row of about ten houses has a communal backyard, which those inhabitants with a strong sense of territory have tried, ineffectually, to divide into individual patches with chicken wire and rustic fencing. The yard abuts onto a field full of high bleached grass, burnt sorrel and convolvulus. Mrs Maycock's house is still basically that of an early twentieth-century agricultural labourer—white-washed walls, gaslight, dusty velvet, black metal, scrubbed deal table, cracked flagstones. Mrs Maycock is small, arthritic, and not very mobile. She admits that her life is bounded by trivial and in-substantial details. Her husband died over thirty years ago; her son lives in Portsmouth. She lives on her old-age pension, with a small supplement. I asked her if she would tell me about her day.

I don't do much. I grow older. Very boring my day. Long as well. I'm awake by four o' clock, and these summer mornings I often get up and make a cup of tea. If it's warm I open the back door and watch the sky get light. Early in the morning — I don't know if you've ever seen it — the sky's all grey, everything's grey. But once the sky gets its colour, the flowers wake up, the snapdragons and the phlox come out of their sleep. That's how I think of it anyway. Some-times I go back to bed if it's wet or if the sun's not shining, but I'm never in bed after seven o'clock. I empty the teapot down the drain out the back, and then make another cup of tea. I hear the men going to work. I hear bits of their conversation, they swear a lot. Still, I think I'd swear if I had to get up every morning of my life and go to work. I know nearly everybody by sight who goes past here. There's one old chap, he must be a piece over eighty, he still works, you can set your watch by him. I used to light my fire and do the grate, but that's all gone now I've got the gas-fire. I miss a coal fire though. I liked the sparks and the flames and the noise. It was company. I have the gas-fire on in the morning for an hour, even in summer. I feel the cold. By eight o'clock I feel time's getting on, the day's getting on. For a lot of people I know it's only just starting, but for me it's practically the middle of the day. I don't get above four or five hours sleep a night. I shall have plenty of time for sleeping soon. It's funny, I lost my husband thirty-two years ago. It seems a lifetime without him. Sometimes I think I've had two lives, one with him and one without him. I'm lucky in a way, I've been two people.

I still do my housework. I make the bed. I always strip it right down, I roll the sheets back, give it an airing. I do a bit of dusting, the dust's terrible in here in the summer. If you were to look at my window-ledge I bet you'd think Oh she isn't half lazy, she never touches her window-ledge. But I've done it this morning. The wind comes in through the cracks, I don't know. This house is like me, going home. Then I do my plants. I love flowers. I don't know what I'd do without flowers. I've got begonias and geraniums. I like primulas and I like a fuchsia. But there's a lot of things I don't get on with. A lot of things you see in the shops, do you know what I think, I saw something in the flower shop on the square, I thought to myself, 'It looks like somebody's inside on a stalk.' Isn't that terrible? But it did. All fleshy. Horrible! I like geraniums, the old-fashioned sort, red and plain.

Then I clean up. I wash the breakfast things. I mop the kitchen floor twice a week. I might rinse a pair of stockings through, hang them on the line. I don't wash sheets now, the man from the laundry comes once a fortnight. They're heavy when they're full of water. Then there's the most exciting part of my day comes next. That's when I go out shopping. I don't buy much because I can't afford it, but it's an outing. I feel it's a real adventure. I tell myself I'm lucky to be able to walk at all. I have a stick, and if it's wet I take it. If there's snow on the ground I'm a bit scared, but I nearly always get out as far as the shops. Of course it means I buy only bits of things, and that works out much more expensive than if you're buying a quantity of something. If I buy meat, a chop or some pork cuttings, it comes to three shillings a time. I have eggs two or three days a week, and Mondays I always have cheese. I'm going to tell you something terrible. I have meals on wheels two days a week, but since the price of meat's gone up they're not very nice. I give most of them to my cat. I know it's terrible, but I don't fancy them any more.

Cheese used to be a real poverty-stricken meal, but it's not now. When my husband was alive I always used to have a roast on Sundays with baked pudding, and I did keep on with it for a time, but I found I was eating it cold on Mondays and Tuesdays as well sometimes, and I got tired of it. I couldn't throw it away, I'd never throw food away. My mother always said it was feeding the devil.

When you get to my age it doesn't take much to interest you. I talk to some of the women in the Co-Op, and the girl in the fruit shop seems a nice little person, although of course there's always a shop full of people. She's very good to me. She'll always put an extra apple on the scales. I say to her 'Are they hard? I don't get on too well with my teeth.'

What do you want to know about my life for? There's nothing goes on in it. I eat beans till the brussels start, then I should think I have brussels nearly every day in the winter. Ern used to grow his own, handsome, hard as nuts they were. There was a person over the road, she used to come and have a bit of dinner with me, but she got very demanding. She stayed for her tea as well, and I had to ask her to go in the end. She even used to come and say what she fancied for her dinner. She doesn't talk to me now. It seems silly, we're both on our own, we could be a bit of company for each other. But she just says 'Good morning' and sometimes she doesn't even say that. I think she must be a bit mental, you don't go into somebody's house and sit there day after day. She's got a lovely house as a matter of fact, and she's much better off than I am. Her husband left her a fair bit of money. He worked down the electric light, they were ever so comfortable. So I don't have any visitors now, not regular visitors.

My son and his wife live down Portsmouth. They come sometimes, but they only stay a night or two, because the grandchildren won't put up with sleeping here. Mind you, they have my bed, and I sleep in the chair down here, but they're not used to sharing a bed. I say sometimes 'You're lucky, I shared a bed with three others when I was a girl!' All dead now. I go down to them for a week in the summer; he comes and fetches me in his car, but I never think you're at ease in other people's houses. And a daughter-in-law can be very funny. They have their different ways. I don't say she's a bad girl, she looks after the kids lovely, but she wants to be dressing up all the while and going out, and when I go down there of course she's got a baby-sitter for nothing, and she's out six nights out of seven. Dancing. When you're thirty-six do you think it's right to want to be off dancing? I don't. I like to go down there, but I'm always glad to get back to my own little house. As long as I've got my health I can't grumble. I go down on my knees and thank God I can still fend for myself. I can put up with being on my own. That's my cross. They say we all have our cross to bear, and that's mine. I've a good neighbour. He works on the railway, and I say 'Hello' to him when he goes to work. He says 'Hello Mrs Maycock', I say 'I wish I could come with you' He says 'All right, you can walk in front of the train with a red flag.' He takes my ash-box out for me on Mondays.

But shopping is the only real outing I get. I watch them on the TV next door sometimes, the politicians. They tell you to shop around, compare the prices. I was going to write to them, how can they expect you to go round and compare prices when it takes you all your time to get to the nearest shop? I bet they've never thought of that. As it happens I'm lucky, our local shopkeepers are quite good, but I do know of old people who pay nearly twice as much because the shop people know they can't go any farther afield and they can open their mouths as wide as they like and know they've got to pay or go without.

I have a rest after dinner. I put my feet up and read the paper. I read the *Express*. I think it's very forthright. I have a doze sometimes, sometimes I don't. Then I get up and have a cup of tea. Molly comes in from next door some days, but she never stays more than about a quarter of an hour. I can't blame her, I've got nothing to say that she'll be interested in. Then the children come home from school. I watch them, they are destructive little devils. Look what they've done to that tree over there. I rap the window to them; they don't take any notice. It seems they don't know what to do with themselves. Then the men start to come home from work. They always look tired. I know he works hard next door. They go to work in the dark and they come home in the dark, that's the way it was when I was a girl and that's the way it is now. So how are we all that better off? I've always been Labour, but I don't vote since Ern died. I don't bother. He was always a big Labour man.

The evenings are the worst. You feel cut off. I shut my back door at five o'clock and that's it for the night. I know nobody'll come. Sometimes they come for the envelopes for charity, but apart from that I know I shan't see anybody till the next morning. I sometimes wonder what would happen if I had a fall. I could just lay here all night and nobody would know. I don't think anybody cares all that much. I wish Terry didn't live down South. If things were different, I could live with them, but not with her being like she is. We should fall out. I think the wireless has been the biggest godsend to me. I think without it I'd've gone mad. I keep it on all the time, even when I'm not listening. It's company. I should prefer somebody to talk to, but beggars can't be choosers can they?

Paul Collins

Paul Collins is thirty. He has done a variety of casual, badly-paid jobs and has lived for five months in a bed-sitter in North London.

My father died seventeen years ago of muscular dystrophy, seven years after it had been diagnosed.

The first five years of my life were wonderful. My father was generous, in love with my mother. But my first conscious memory of him is his head falling between his shoulders in a gesture of defeat, with a gasping outlet of breath. My aunt said 'You worked too hard on the path Reg.'; he'd been building a concrete garden path. That was when we learned that he had progressive muscular dystrophy, that there was no hope, that he had between seven and fourteen years to live. It was in 1946. We had just won the war and he was just about to launch himself into a career in higher technology; he'd begun to furnish the house. For three months they had the only telephone in the entire neighbourhood, and then they had to have it removed. My mother was bursting with confidence and pride in Reg. He was brilliant. But it destroyed them both before he died. When they knew he had dystrophy, everything collapsed. My boyhood from five till twelve was seven years' death.

Once we went to the river, and he sailed a metal boat he'd made, with a methylated spirits engine. I felt strange, recalling a strong Daddy in the past, by expecting *this* Daddy almost deliberately to sabotage it; and, lo and behold, the boat sailed off into the chickweed and some boys on the opposite bank sank it with stones. He never really tried to stop them, although he pretended to. The boat had been made before his sickness — same as I had this great model railway in the garden, a huge white rabbit in a green hutch, a goldfish in a large fish-tank with an aerator, and the radio sets he'd made and the electric alarm clock that woke you up at the right time, switched the radio on and boiled the kettle. The garden was full of flowers; he put a gate upstairs to stop me falling down; everything was brightly painted, we had a chiming gong for the front doorbell, a large wire letter box, a new white telephone; there was tiled fireplaces, a veneer sideboard, a chiming clock. He was planning to buy a motor-car and to make his own TV set. He kept a scrap-album of drawings he'd encouraged me to do; there was a model wooden galleon-ship that he'd made. Then he built a coal-bunker and a concrete back-yard, and he'd started on the concrete path when he collapsed and the hospital diagnosed muscular dystrophy.

As a child I was withdrawn, passive, deprived and shaken. I'd been taught to admire him in my first five years and so modelled myself on him during the next seven, which was fatal, since under dystrophy he was the opposite of his true self, so I finished up with a muscular-dystrophy personality; certain sub-conscious assumptions, such as that my Dad was a great man, even though he never did anything but sit in a chair all his life and never achieved anything. So I could be great by doing nothing and being a failure (indeed, had a sacred duty to do so).

They had promised me so much when I was a baby, and actually I was then given death and horror. I felt resentful, lost, retarded. I wet the bed until I was eleven, and he spoke to me about it once, because it caused Mother so much work; then there was the asthma, for which I had to go to health-school when I was ten. The house that had been a space-rocket was suddenly a haunted tomb.

At his, my father's final Christmas party, when his face was so affected by the ravages of dystrophy, he wore plastic spectacles and a nose-piece to conceal it from the guests.

The last excursion with my father was to see an aunt and uncle. There had been a quarrel; the visit was to make things up. There was a tiny fire and sandwiches with the slightest coating of fish-paste. My father kept his overcoat on; he was far gone and never said a word all evening. Then we went home, and this involved negotiating a long, straight, steeply sloping hill to the bus-stop; it was late, not a soul in

sight, yellow neon lighting. He got halfway up, so
slowly that it was frankly exasperating and then he
stopped. For the first time in her life, my mother
dared to rebel against Reg. She said angrily 'No, don't
give up. Come on.' Tears rolled down his cheeks and
he said 'You don't know what it's like'. She said 'Yes
I do. Come on' aggressively, and he had to continue
without a rest, leaning on his walking stick and his
wife, in the midst of dystrophy-suffocation. It was
manifestly the last time that he would venture out.
The next-door neighbour thought he was malingering,
because he could still 'potter about'; and he harassed
us in a minor way — tipped refuse on our front garden pathway; complained that our sewing-machine
needed a suppressor as it was interfering with his TV
reception. After my father died, he began to feel perhaps there'd been a flaw in his logic, and he apolo-
gised. 'I'm *ever* so sorry Mrs Collins, *Whatever* was the
matter with him?' My mother said 'Well it's too late
now Jim, he's gone.'

My childhood was a death-camp. I've been
haunted, lost and nihilistic ever since. I've wandered.
I've been on a tour of the whole world, literally, even
that was perhaps a flight from my nightmare father.
There was more to it than 'Daddy-sick' — that's in-
adequate to explain the full extent of my suffering,
deprivation, neurosis, confusion, masochism, self-
torment, inadequacy, ostracism. No, those two
people who functioned as my parents, thought I was
the devil. My mother married again, and she treated
me with ruthless, incessant and inexhaustible bully-
ing; instead of trying to compensate for the nightmare I'd been through by providing an intelligent
home-life, she reacted more as one would to a pitiable
demon who needs exorcising.

They believed I was the jinx or destroying spirit
from the supernatural world. I've always been dis-
turbed about something ill-defined, and now I'm
thirty I'm sure *that's* it. I wasn't just deprived from
five onwards, I was secretly hated.

I'm thirty, in a furnished room, alone, and when I
work, labouring in the lowest-paid unskilled jobs. I've

never established a permanent relationship with a woman.

I failed the eleven-plus, left school at fifteen, went into an engineering apprenticeship which I didn't finish; drifted. I'm drifting still.

Miss Quentin

Miss Quentin is in her late fifties and lives alone in a detached bungalow in a London suburb; the roof is low and the tiles are covered with pale moss and lichen; the front wall is almost entirely covered with ornamental trees. The structure of the bungalow is concealed by plants and trees; everything is reticence, timidity and concealment.

Miss Quentin is a small, attractive woman who is nervous. She wears a long black skirt, silver-threaded slippers, and a wrap that is half-stole, half-shawl, over a modern print blouse. Tea is laid out on hexagonal plates covered with brown and orange designs — sandwiches, bread and butter, cake. In the grate, a gleaming and symmetrical pyramid of half-burnt coals. Low armchairs with floral covers, beams, wooden lamp with parchment frame and low-watt bulb; everywhere there are pictures of Miss Quentin's family: smiling, posed, on holiday, relaxed. Miss Quentin is silent at first; the sound of the coals burning with a faint metallic crackle. Miss Quentin had expected to meet an older man; she is not convinced that I will understand.

Being lonely is to be aware that there is no one living who knows you; who can say 'Oh that's just like you' when you say something, or 'That's not you at all.' Within five years I lost my darling mother, my brother and a sweetheart. While my mother was alive, I used to keep a record of all the things that happened in a diary. When I read it now, I can't believe it's the same person. When someone who is so close to you dies, you lose part of yourself. To think there's nobody who can anticipate your moods, nobody who cares. Of course, there is a part of oneself that one would never reveal to anyone, except perhaps one's Maker; and one still has friends; but it isn't the same as those who know one intimately. I was so happy with my mother. We were more like sisters. Only one thing I'm thankful for, she didn't suffer, she died in her sleep.

We came to this house forty-six years ago, when it was new; and all my parents' life is here in it, in the work they did to it. When we came here, the garden was simply a heap of builders' rubble, and we had to spend a year with bare walls until it dried out. People have said to me 'Why don't you move?' But how could I leave all my memories that are here? My family were everything to me. So many small things I miss, the rattle of teacups, sitting by the fire, listening to music. There was no need to talk — simply to share. I never had a sweetheart when I was young. Life seemed so full.

[*Miss Quentin had prepared tea before I arrived; and had stored the sandwiches in the oak sideboard to prevent them from drying up. They were presented daintily with stalks of cress and parsley.*] I like to sit at the table really, but when it's very cold it's good to be by the fire. I think good manners and courtesy are important to make living really gracious. I'm afraid there are so many people who are after money and material things all the time, they have no time to consider others. There's no respect for authority any more.

I've never been abroad, never travelled. I've spent most of my life in this area; although there's the noise from the airport and the traffic. I've always written, poetry, and my journal. Music and poetry have always been a great consolation to me.

I think one of the happiest times of my life was when my mother and I were knitting for the soldiers in the war. We'd sit and listen to the radio, and we felt we were really doing our bit. We used to slip a note into the gloves or socks or whatever it was, just a note to say 'I hope these keep you warm'. I could talk all day about the memories this house has for me.

Keith Hallam

Keith Hallam is a university student of nineteen. He has shoulder-length hair, rectangular glasses and wears a black and lilac parti-coloured jacket and flared denim trousers. It is a wet Saturday night. The bright arc of light-bulbs of an amusement arcade in central London is mirrored smudgily in the wet pavement. Keith is damp and forlorn, and exudes an air of quiet despair.

I don't know why it's called gay, I think it's the most miserable thing in the world. I've known I was, ever since I was about thirteen or fourteen, but it was only when I came to London last year that I was able to express myself sexually. The trouble is that it's prevented me from doing anything else, work especially. I haven't done enough work. I've just done my exams, I expect I've failed. It's a mistake to think that being liberated means getting all the sexual experience you can. There has to be some kind of balance. If I fail, I shall have to leave university. I don't know what I'll do then. I don't know how homosexuals form relationships. I don't have any. Of all the people I've met this year, I should think only one or two have wanted to see me again, and they're always the ones I didn't particularly like. I've been into drugs, only the soft ones, but that's an isolating experience too. I don't have any friends at college, and sharing drug experiences with them isn't my idea of what a relationship should be. I know I'm quite attractive superficially; a lot of people are interested in me, but it always wears off when they find out what I'm really like.

I'm a classic case really. My mother wanted a girl. We're working-class. I'm the apple of my mother's eye, which makes me sad. It's a kind of responsibility I can't live up to. Sometimes I stop and think that what I do is against the law, as I'm under twenty-one. I don't worry about that — I find it difficult enough to get by from day to day, without adding to my anxieties by stupid things like that. Before I came to

London, I had all these fantasies about finding myself and being free to associate with whoever I chose. It's turned out to be something else. It's a kind of compulsion — the more sex you have, the more you think you need. If you ever find yourself on your own — and I do an awful lot of the time — there's only one thing to do, and that's go and look for someone to pick up. You can sleep with as many people as you like, and still be lonely as hell. Going back home on the night buses, lying awake on the edge of somebody's single bed waiting till the tubes start so you can get out, making vague promises to meet again, people you can't stand the sight of the next morning. You eat perfunctory breakfasts and say unenthusiastic hellos to other people's flatmates, a succession of faceless Adrians and Peters and Julians. It's no way to live, honestly.

Mrs Ellis

*Mrs Ellis is about forty-two and lives on a council
estate in south-east London. There is an abandoned
car outside Mrs Ellis's house, rusting and swarming
with children. Many of the privet hedges around the
houses are overgrown. In some of the front gardens
the grass is rank and uncared for; in others it has
been worn away into a muddy depression in the
earth. Several of the panes of glass in the downstairs
window are broken, and have been replaced with
pieces of cardboard—not bare, but neatly covered
by wallpaper. All the curtains downstairs are drawn,
and bare light bulbs are burning in the kitchen and
the living room. The side door has been recently
repainted; but the paint is already chipped where it
has been kicked and is muddy with the smudged
marks of dogs' paws.*

*Mrs Ellis is a pleasant and mild-tempered woman,
very good-looking, but already faded. She has
recently acquired a 'best room.' Newly papered by
the Council in a pattern of green Regency stripes and
medallions, and with some linoleum in an orange
simulation of mosaic.*

*The first time I met Mrs Ellis, she had just been
cutting out shilling-size shapes from a piece of old
linoleum, for insertion in the gas-meter. When she
was in debt, she frequently emptied the meters; the
gas and electricity have been cut off several times in
the past few years. Public officials—Social Security,
gas board men, health visitors, housing workers—
talk about her with a kind of scornful weariness: she
is one of the crosses they have to bear.*

I haven't touched the meters for ages. I wouldn't, not
now... Life isn't easy though. Graham and Joanie's
working now, and so's their Dad. He's driving for a
building firm, and Graham works with him. Joanie's
in the laundry. It's a job, but she don't get much
money. I tell her, 'You want to stick it, it's security,
there's always plenty of dirt to be washed, no shortage of dirt!' So we have enough to buy food these
days, which is something. No extras though. I like a

smoke, and sometimes we go out on Saturday night for a drink. Only one, because that's all we can afford. Apart from that I don't go out. I meet the kids out of school, and I do a bit of shopping, but I don't go anywhere else. I haven't had a holiday, not since — well, since before I was married — I'd love to see the sea.

I don't talk to anybody round here much. They're all ever so snobbish, look down on you if you've got a few kids. Her next door — well — I mean, I do swear at my kids if they don't behave theirselves, you do, don't you? But she comes out and starts making me feel small. But you've got to control your kids, haven't you, else they start controlling you. People round here think they're better than what we are.

I don't want to get too thick with them anyway, get to know all your business. That's why I don't go to Bingo. I've got the kids, that's enough for me. Kathie's married now, she lives down Woolwich. I go and see her sometimes. They've only got one room, but they're on the housing list... [*Mrs Ellis shows me a child of about one year, sleeping in a pram.*] This is Dean, my youngest. I went to be — seen to like, so I couldn't have any more babies. And then I went and fell for another. His Dad says he sneaked in where he shouldn't. I thought I was pregnant, only I thought no it can't be. I got really worried, I thought I must have cancer. And then I started to get really big, so I knew I was all right. I was ever so bad having him though. I had haemorrhage for twenty-six days; took me months to get over it.

I does my shopping in the morning, then I comes back here and then Joanie comes in for her dinner, then I gets Dean to sleep, and by that time the others come home from school and that's your day gone. I had a lady come to see me from the Welfare. She was nice, but they say they're going to do this and do the other for you, then they forget all about you...

I come from a big family myself, only I don't know where they all are. My brother, he lives down Greenwich. I think he's got money. He must have, otherwise he'd come to see us. I did have a sister round the corner, only she moved three years ago, and we ain't heard from her since. Kathie come in one dinner time, she said she might go down to Bassey Down [*Basildon*] to live. Up North. I said to her 'You won't like it after London'. But it's her life, she can do what she wants with it. I sometimes wonder what I'll do when all the kids've gone. I like big families. People should stick together but they don't.

Social workers who have known Mrs Ellis for a long time say she is only really happy when she is pregnant. As soon as the child arrives, she cannot cope; but during pregnancy she expands and flourishes. She loves her children and is loyal to them and to her husband. She admits to petty pilfering from shops as well as to depredations on the property of the Gas Board, but says 'I'd do anything for my kids, I'd never let them want. I'd sooner go to prison than see them go short.' Three of her children were at Special Schools for the educationally subnormal; one is in the remedial stream of a Comprehensive; one in junior school; two are below school age.

Mrs Ellis has been exposed to view by the raised living standards of the working class. Where she was once concealed, she is suddenly and painfully in evidence, demanded to give an account of herself; no less an object of contempt to her working-class neighbours than to those for whom she represents idleness, fecklessness and irresponsibility. What she suffers from is really a quite neutral affliction — limited ability and lack of mental endowment to cope with the complex demands of consumerist society.

Derrick

Derrick is about forty. He admits to being ugly. He is short and bald and has a stammer and a slight limp. He has worked as a milkman, bus-conductor and casual labourer—jobs without skill or security. He is unmarried and lives in lodgings in a house kept by a widow of seventy-five who can scarcely cope. There is threadbare linoleum on the floor of Derrick's single room, with a small brown and orange carpet with a zigzag design; a bed with a very greasy and faded candlewick bedspread. The room was last papered in the fifties—reeds and grasses on a beige background. There is a shiny bulky wardrobe. Its door is open, showing bundles of crumpled clothes, shirts, grey flannels, overalls. Derrick's parents separated when he was very young, and he was brought up by a grandmother. He has no personal relationships of any kind. As a result, he claims he is an expert on the art of masturbation.

You can tell what it's going to be like before you even start. It can depend on all sorts of circumstances — how full your bladder is, how tired you are, how long it takes to get hard. Some days it feels different, — some days it's hard and bony, others it's like rubber. Sometimes you hardly notice when you've finished, other times it shakes you right through. I do it at least once every day I should think. If it's bad, it can put you in a bad mood for the whole day, because you know it's the highlight of the day, and once it's over, there's nothing else to look forward to, except perhaps a bit of grub. I don't think about women, other people in that way. Not me. They're a million miles away, walking down the street. I see these girls, I never think of them when I walk past them in the street. I have a look, that's all, but I think of them, remember them for when I'm on my own. You see pictures of them in your mind, some days very sexy, other days you can't think of a single one while you're doing it. That's frustrating as well. I have had women when I was younger. I had a girl who worked in a factory, well-built, not bad at all. We went up Victoria Park, in the bushes there, it was grand. But I found out that she only went with me because she'd never done it before, and she'd got a bloke that she didn't want to know she was a virgin. So she tried it out on me. An experiment. I could've killed her. If I had the chance of doing it with a woman now, I don't even know I'd take it. I wouldn't know what to do. Well, I'd know what to do like, only I'd be embarrassed. I wouldn't know what to say to her, before and afterwards. Might be all right if she was deaf and dumb.

I think of myself as being outside, apart. I don't envy other people. I just think it's all got nothing to do with me, it's not my business. When I see people walking arm in arm, in love, whatever they call it, I just know I'm not one of those it's ever going to happen to. One thing you do notice, the papers are full of sex and drugs. Everybody's doing it. Well I'm not. It doesn't affect people like me. I don't count. I'm not alone, there must be thousands like me. Sometimes I see Mrs Hassell's TV, the adverts. Where do all the people in them live? I never see them. I could be bitter about it, but it wouldn't do any good. The only one who'd suffer'd be me. It's no good having a chip on your shoulder. I might win the pools, then I'd be able to buy all the sex and love I need. I think everybody, they talk about love, but it's only for what they can get out of each other. Everybody exploits somebody, don't they? Nobody cares about anybody but themselves when the cards are down. If I work for a bloke, say, and he pays me a wage, well he must be able to make a profit, mustn't he, or he wouldn't be in business. So it stands to reason he doesn't pay me the amount my labour's worth. He has to underpay, or there'd be no profit. That's exploitation.

If you passed me by in the street, what would you think of me? You probably wouldn't even notice me. You might just glance at me and think 'Oh thank God I'm not like that.' People do. You can tell by the way their eyes move away if you catch them looking. If you look a bit... ugly, people think you have no intelligence either. They sometimes talk to you as if you were simple, you know, shout, or talk slow. They make conclusions from the way you look. I've sat in the park, and I've heard women, mothers, call their children away from me if they've been playing near the bench where I'm sitting. You might think I'm exaggerating, but I know. They don't trust me. They think 'Hello, what's he doing, sitting in the park when all decent people are at work. He's going to offer my kid sweets in a minute, and the next I know, he'll be doing things to them.' I'm intelligent. I watch people. There's a lot goes on in my mind. People who look at me as if I was something from outer space would be surprised.

I never knew my parents. Well I knew my mother by sight. She was more of an acquaintance than anything. I lived with my Gran. We lived up Croxton Gardens, and my mother used to call once a month, kiss me, swallow a cup of tea and then go away again. Once I saw her in the street with a man. I said to my Gran, 'Is that my Dad?' She said 'No, it's a friend of your mother's.' She didn't care about me; I didn't kid myself she did. I used to hate her. I blamed her, because I'd got one leg longer than the other. She caused it all I used to think. She made me ugly and small by not loving me. In a way I reckon I was right. She made me ugly and small inside as well as out.

Jean Pritchard

*Jean Pritchard is thirty-eight and lives alone in a
bedsitter in Lewisham. She had recently separated
from her husband and works as a clerical assistant.*

I was married when I was eighteen. That was the
biggest mistake of all. What can anybody know about
the world when they're eighteen? I wanted to get
away from home. I thought my parents had made a
mess of their lives, I was convinced I could do better.
I didn't, I did a damn sight worse. My parents should
never have stayed together really. My Mum used to
like to go out and have a good time, but the old man
wanted to stay at home all the while. Opposite to
most people, it's nearly always the man who likes to
go out and the woman who stops at home.

My mother used to resent me. I was a rival to her,
because she always dressed ever so young, and she
used to be pleased as punch when anybody said to
her 'Oh you're far too young to have a daughter that
age.' In fact, there was a time when she went round
telling people I was her half-sister, but most of the
people round us knew us from way back and they
knew it wasn't true. She used to dress up, take me
out, but when we were alone I could never do a thing
right. When I was a bit older she used to blame me for
causing her to lose her figure, and she used to talk
about carrying me in her belly and giving me birth as
if she'd done me a great big favour. My father was
fifteen years older than she was. He got Parkinson's
and went all shaky, and could hardly walk. She got
impatient with him and said he was like it on purpose. I hated my childhood. I hated him because he
was so old and I was ashamed of her because she tried
to act like a kid all the time.

We lived in this flat in Lewisham, really run-down
and tatty, not been painted for years. It was at the
top of the house, which was terrible for the old man,
but she said things like she'd rather die than live in a
council flat, and other people provided houses for
their families, why couldn't he.

When I was seventeen, two doors away there was four young blokes living together. They'd got cars, they looked student types, and that gave her something else to moan about because they had parties and played jazz records. Anyway, one of these young fellows, I thought he was fantastic. I used to hang about, trying to get him to look at me. He did notice me in the end. My God he did. He was gorgeous. You may think it's peculiar, but I'd never met many boys, in the sense of boy-friends. I thought about it all the time, I think all teenage girls do, but in the factory, at school I never really thought of them as my type. I think some of the old lady's bullshit about making the most of yourself — that was one of her sayings 'Make the most of yourself': she really meant being snobbish and make out you're something you're not — I must have taken some of it in without realising it. She liked to think she was 'refined'. I hated her. I always swore I'd never be like her, and I used to deliberately act common and talk really London, which made her mad.

Peter was training to be an accountant. We couldn't have been more different. His family lived in Lincolnshire, his father was a farmer. And Peter took me out, and he really liked me. I couldn't believe it. I thought 'Wow, this has got to end, this can't be happening to me, there's got to be a catch in it somewhere.' I wasn't clever or anything, but I'm very lively. I know I was attractive. I'm not blowing my own trumpet. I know I might have been a brainless bitch, but I knew how to use what I had got. I didn't need the old lady's tuition for that. One weekend we went up to Grantham to meet his parents. They liked me, his father especially. I told them I was working temporarily in the bottling, to get experience, and what I really wanted to do was to take a course and be a confectioner, something creative. They thought I was a nice girl, ambitious, not backward, but not too pushing either. I told them that my father was disabled by illness and my mother was a saint, struggling on bravely. I was a bitch, the lies I told them, and they were all sympathy. Well I don't think his mother was all that impressed, actually. I think she thought I was after her boy, and she'd probably have liked somebody out of the local gymkhana kind of thing, but she didn't show it. She was very polite.

We got married. They gave him a house, furnished, and a car, and he was still only training. They thought we ought to have waited, but I got pregnant, and our old lady got all excited. She thought I ought to grab him before he slipped through my fingers. We went to live in Kent, where he could commute to work every day. Great. The only trouble was that my life came to a full stop on the day I got married. You might think, 'Oh well, it doesn't sound as if it was any great shakes anyway'; but I was very independent minded, and all that had to go. My wedding day was like other people's funerals. I buried my own personality.

He was my lord and master. My own parents had always been at each other's throats; my mother had tried to dominate everybody, and that really screwed me up. So I decided whatever happened my kids were going to have security, love and all that; and I vowed I'd never row with Peter in front of them. And I didn't. I let him dictate everything to me, the way to bring them up, schools to send them to, although I hated the idea of prep school for John. I depended on him, him and his family had given me everything, I felt they know best, because my old lady's rubbish, let's face it. But the sick thing is the kids have grown up into real snobs. They take one look at my old lady. They think she's really comic, you know she doesn't have any teeth and she tries to talk posh, and it sounds as if she's trying to whistle. I know she's been an old sod, but she's old now, and she's a bit pathetic. It makes me wild to see them take the piss. I hate them. I hate my own kids. The old lady loves being patronised, she thinks they're real class. John is a little gentleman. Well it's not true, I don't hate them, but I despise their snobbishness. And it all comes from Peter. Isn't it funny, you're so busy trying not to be like your own parents you turn into something just as bad without realising it. I think deep down he felt he'd let himself down. He never said it. There was no need. In fact, even today he's more dependent on me than I am on him, emotionally.

Of course I lapped it all up at first. Who wouldn't? I'd never had a good home, material comforts, so I accepted everything that went with them. Being polite, being Conservative. I did resent it, that they automatically expected you were Conservative. I thought 'Oh well, they must be right, they've got on, they're well to do, they understand things better, they must be right.' The only time I ever had an argument was about the railwaymen. There was a rail strike once and Peter was going on about the railway workers; and of course my old man had been on the railways, and I just thought of him going out at six in the morning with an enamel tea-can in one hand, a hunk of bread and two cold sausages in a paper bag, and I went mad. I said 'You ignorant bastard, you know sod-all about it.' That was a mistake of course. He said 'Don't you ever talk to me like that again'; and I felt ashamed, because that only convinced him, not that I was right in my argument, but just that I came from rubbish. But that was the only time I ever had a political discussion with him. I let him get away with it the rest of the time. He was shocked to find I had an idea in my head. Because the women on the estates where we've lived, oh you wouldn't believe it. Take the dog for a walk, go to town for lunch, have their hair done, pour tea and wait for hubby to come home so they can wheedle the price of a new hat out of him. And when their husbands come home, they talk to them like somebody they've just met at a cocktail party. Peter expected me to be the same. I was, I ought to have been an actress really. There's some parts I'm perfect at. I was a good hostess. I could cook and serve up dinner for eight, and sit down and look cool, and they always said 'Isn't she marvellous'. I learned to talk about nothing, cooking, flowers, travel.

After two or three years I just fell out of love with him. I didn't hate him, but I despised the way he was. He had no imagination, he lived this terrible routine, he said the same things every day. He was middle-aged at twenty-six. He was still quite attractive, but he'd settled into a monotonous way of living that obviously he expected to carry on till the day he died, or retired, whichever came first. I knew by the time I was twenty-two that I would wait for my kids to start work, or leave school, and then I'd leave him. I would have had a lover, except the only men I ever came across were as boring and futile as he was. And that's just what I did. I walked out on them just over eighteen months ago. I got myself a flat, and he came home one night and I said 'I'm going to live in a flat in Lewisham' and he said 'Oh?' and I said 'Yes, I'm going next week.' I walked out. I'd waited years to do it. I don't have a scrap of regret. It's a bit of an anti-climax, but it's the only thing I've ever done in my life that I wanted to do and that wasn't dictated by somebody else. I should never have married a bloke like that if it hadn't been for my mother's influence. I'm lonely now sometimes. It's different from the loneliness of the years I spent in that house. I even talk about them as though they were nothing to do with me. They weren't. When I left Peter said 'What about your children?' And I said 'No Peter, they're yours, like everything in our life.' They think I've gone mental.

[*Jean began to cry; I suggested we might talk about something else. She said 'Why, are you embarrassed? I'm not,' and then laughed.*]

They must think I'm mental. That's the only ex-planation for walking out on all that, the wonderful home, the colour TV, Rover 2000. It isn't easy. If I hadn't promised myself for fifteen years it was what I was going to do, I don't know where I'd have got the courage from. It isn't easy to start again with people at my age, although I do have friends, boy-friends as well. But at least my loneliness is *my* loneliness now. I don't have it forced on me by other people. And I regard that as an improvement. If I get married again, if I have any real deep relationship with other people, it'll be because I choose to do it. Funny, I don't have any feeling of responsibility or duty to any of them, except my old man, and he died in 1961.

Mr Appleby

Mr Appleby is a widower in his mid-forties. He is the housekeeper in a home for lonely people run by a private charity. He is friendly and communicative and at first gives little indication of the chain of events which brought him to this unlikely place. He drinks coffee from a mug with a Scorpio on it, but I, being a guest, have a cup and saucer. The room is light, uncluttered, warm. Mr Appleby tells his story, starkly, openly.

He lost his whole family in a car crash two years ago. He had been driving up to Luton to see his mother one Sunday morning: they had left the motorway just past St Albans to stop for some coffee. In the car were his wife, his twin boys and their two dogs. A pantechnicon collided with the offside of the car; his wife was thrown through the windscreen, his boys were killed at once by the shattered metal. He himself was thrown on to the grass verge some yards away.

He was unconscious for three weeks. He has a vague recollection of having been transferred from St Albans to Charing Cross hospital in an ambulance, a journey which, he was later told, had been accomplished in twelve minutes with police escort because of the seriousness of his injuries. He remained for a long time in an intensive care unit, and after some weeks it became clear that he was not going to die.

He says that his case became quite celebrated. He has been referred to in medical journals and visited by many specialists; a lot of the doctors and nurses who attended him called him 'Mr Miracle,' not only because he managed to survive at all, but because of the indomitability and cheerfulness with which he did so. His arm and leg had both been broken by the accident; the right side of his body badly crushed; the whole abdomen severely damaged. He has no kidney, no bladder, only a vestigial penis. He says jokingly that without the filters and plates and iron-mongery inside him, he weighs next to nothing. He still visits hospital every few weeks to have the penis dilated, so that it doesn't become blocked entirely.

He says that the doctors were anxious to see whether he was still capable of sexual feeling: whether there was any pain or discomfort in a situation of arousal. They sent his favourite nurse to dress him, and he could see her breasts through the carefully contrived décolletage. The doctors asked his reaction. Nothing. This had apparently been the right answer, because if he had felt any sensation, this would have meant yet another major operation.

He was in hospital twelve months. After a long period of convalescence, someone from a private charity suggested he might try a period in one of their homes. In the new environment, Mr Appleby found a new reason for living, and soon became housekeeper of one of the homes. At present there are four other lonely (or perhaps formerly lonely) people in the house, all with different problems; Mr Appleby discovered that he has an intuitive feeling for social work. The group operates as a family. Each member pays L8 a week; some are working, some receive social security; but it is still more secure, more humane and cheaper than any institution. On the previous day Mr Appleby had taken some of the children from next door to the pantomime in Lewisham. There is a good relationship with most of the neighbours.

I get up early. I must be the only man in London who's never in bed after five o'clock in the morning. I might do some cleaning, have a cup of tea. By half-past-nine I've been to the shops and come back. I cook one meal a day, a hot meal at night, which we try and have all together. Some days I do have a bad turn, and have to rest, but I get over it.

It's given me a new lease of life this place. Some of the people, if they didn't have these homes to come to, well I don't know where they'd be. Although I've lost so much, I'm still capable of feelings. I'm fond of the people here. I could cuddle anybody, show them affection like, but it would be all the same, whoever it was, if it was you or Greta Garbo, a film-star, it'd be all the same.

I think the reason I've survived is will-power. I've got the will to live, and I've discovered I can help other people. I've been offered compensation for the accident. A lot of money. My case was heard in the High Court, by the Master of the Rolls, Lord Denning. He was very fair. I'm pleased about it, of course, but you can't compensate for things like that. I shall give some of it to the home. Your life can never be the same; I can't hear, you see, I've no hearing at all in this ear, and I've the hearing aid in the other. I've only one tooth left; I had all my own teeth. I've a plate here in my arm, as well as the filters. There's lots of things I have to do in private, that's why I have to have my own room of course. But I'm still here. There is hope. You might have thought I'd never recover, a lot of people wouldn't have. But you've got to have hope and faith in yourself. You've got to know that other people care about you and that you care for them.

Maud & Irene

Maud, who is eighty-nine, lost her husband six years ago. She and her daughter Irene, who is sixty-four, live off old age pensions and supplementary benefit. They rent a ramshackle house in the derelict inner area of a Midland town, once a prosperous middle-class dwelling. Mother and daughter have retreated into the warm back kitchen: the rest of the house is neglected, bare and dusty. The hall is cavernous: the moulding of acorns and oak-leaves is obscured by a frail and intermittent fabric of cobwebs. The wall-paper is dark, and the motif of dense wreaths of maroon vine-leaves scarcely distinguishable. On a plank nailed to the wall are some black-painted S-hooks, from which hang an old sports coat and a greasy gabardine raincoat which belonged to the old woman's husband.

The kitchen itself is a small dark room; and its single sash-window looks on to the dingy flaking whitewash of a factory wall. Maud sits in a green leather armchair, much patched, and losing its stuffing here and there. She wears wrinkled stockings, a stained skirt and man's cardigan fastened with a safety-pin. Her hair is thin, and plaited in a loose tail pinned in the nape of her neck. The cardigan is hemmed with grime where she has clutched it with her hand. The graining of the loose skin at her throat is etched with dirt. She is holding a steel comb tangled with wisps of hair.

Irene is sitting at the table covered with news-papers, consulting some racing papers and writing down the names of the horses she fancies on the flap of a used envelope. She wears a black satin dress stained with food, and a brown sweater which belonged to her father. In a cage, roughly made of wood with a front of wire netting, is a white budge-rigar. The bottom of the cage is covered with husks of millet and splashes of dried shit; and some of the millet-seed has spilled out of the netting and on to the floor. In one of the recesses in the wall there are some brown-painted bookshelves, with a copy of Home Doctor *and* Illustrated Encyclopedia, *horo-*

*scope books and racing forecasts, and Woolworth
exercise books in which Irene has written the words
of popular songs of the 1930s and 40s.*

*Maud is very deaf and in order to communicate
Irene has to raise her voice to a shriek, which is such
an effort for her that each time she finishes a
sentence she is left exhausted and trembling. Maud
goes out two or three times a week to the pub over
the road, where there is always someone who will
buy her a drink on the strength of her great age and
indomitability. Apart from these excursions she
doesn't go out at all. She is afraid of the frequent
blackouts and dizzy spells which she has known over
the past two or three years. She will not go to the
doctor because he may find something seriously
wrong with her. Although the house is draughty and
damp, she will not move. The rent is still only 50p a
week, and this leaves her with a little for a drink and
the betting shop. All the time she dwells upon death,
half humorous, half macabre.*

I don't think they want me up there, or down there,
wherever it is. I expect St Peter knows I'm a wicked
old woman. He knows I like a drink and a bob or two
on the horses. Still I don't care about him knowing,
as long as he don't go and tell them at the Assistance.
[*She chuckles*] The worst he can do to me is to strike
me dead, and I'm ready for that. I've been living on
borrowed time for twenty years. Don't want them at
the Assistance to stop me bit of supplementary
though.

[*Irene looks unhappy at her mother's constant
references to death. For her it is too real.*]

It's a full-time job for me now. She won't move
from here. I'd like to get my name down on the
council waiting list for a flat, but she won't shift. I
wonder what'll happen to me when she's gone. Sometimes, when she's gone to bed I hear a bump, I think
'Oh, she's fallen down', and I rush upstairs, my heart
beating like mad, and she says 'What's up with you,
did you think I'd kicked the bucket?' Sometimes she
snores, snorts like, in her sleep in the night, and it

134

sounds just like the death-rattle. Frightens me to death. I'm all the while listening, I never relax. I mean, I know it's got to come, but I've always been a whittler, I worry about it. Although I know I've been lucky in many ways, perhaps I shouldn't grumble. I've had good parents. But I can't go out anywhere, I don't like leaving her. I daren't leave her. I do miss company though. I used to like company. I used to be in the darts team, a lot of things I used to do. You get out of the habit of talking to people, and anyway, when you get to a certain age the young people don't want to know you. I sometimes sit in the pub and listen to people talking, and I think I'd love to join in, I've got a lot of things I could say, but I daren't.

I did have a boy-friend once. Oh, I was getting on, even then, but she swore he was married and wouldn't let me see him. She came down the pub one night when I'd promised to meet him, and she put up such a performance, it made me ashamed. I was over forty then. He wasn't married. Well, I think he was divorced, but that didn't matter to me. Things like that don't matter if you care about somebody, and I did. He wasn't anything special, he'd been in prison. But she wouldn't let me. I should have done what I wanted myself and gone ahead, but I didn't. I was frightened of her. I was very shy, I didn't mix much. I expect she wanted somebody to look after her in her old age. Well, she's been lucky, hasn't she? The only thing is, who have I got, who's going to look after me? Some days I feel I need looking after. I'm not well myself. I have the most terrible constipation, and I get pains all down the veins in my legs, some days I hardly know how to put one leg after the other.

[*Maud looks from Irene to me, nodding and smiling, and making out that she can follow the conversation.*]

I see the price of funerals has gone up. They reckon it's going to cost a hundred pounds just to be buried. Well at that rate I can't afford to die. And I'm damn sure I can't afford to live either, so I don't know what I'm going to do.

Sylvester Mallalieu

Sylvester Mallalieu is a university student of nineteen living off a grant in a flat near the university.

I came to England in 1961 when I was eight. My mother was living in Nottingham, and I was with my grandmother in St Lucia. I was good at school but the teacher we had there was very ignorant and very tough. She tried to stop us talking patois which we resented. I couldn't believe how free it was in the schools here. I was very good at English, I don't know why, because I had parents who really couldn't speak English at all properly. I was lucky, because I went to a good Comprehensive school, and they were so pleased to have a black kid who wasn't remedial. Because I had a spark of intelligence, I was used as an example to all the other black kids: Look at Sylvester, he can do it. I used to hate it. It drove a block between me and the other black kids.

I made friends more easily with the white kids, and quite a few of them took me home. Sometimes their parents were a bit doubtful; they used to shout at me as if I was deaf or couldn't understand English, or even talk to me in pidgin English, 'you no likee' sort of thing. That was very funny. One day I was at my friend's house, and a next door neighbour came in, and she looked at me and said 'Is he all right?' And my friend's mother said 'Oh it's a real pleasure to have him here, he's ever so polite, and he's got lovely manners.' Just as if I wasn't there, or they were talking in a foreign language. She was a kind woman, but she just had no idea of all the assumptions behind what she was saying — surprise that somebody from the trees could be polite, the fact that she could say so without thinking of my feelings. It makes you feel that you're not there all the time. It's disturbing.

I was liked because I was the one living example that proved that THEY could fit in, and that all could be harmony and love. I was completely taken over, I had no identity at all, and I didn't exist except as someone to flatter their liberal prejudices. That was as bad as colonialism mark one. I got to hate Nottingham, and I hated all the other black kids. My parents spoke Creole patois at home, and I couldn't bring myself to use it. I felt so ashamed, and I dreaded anybody — whites — hearing them together, although most whites wouldn't have recognised what it was anyway, and they certainly wouldn't have guessed that it indicated they were ignorant country people.

He wasn't my father, but my mother and he had got two younger kids, and one of them was epileptic. He was a bit slow at learning and my father used to sit him at the table and give him a book and tell him he wouldn't get anything to eat until he'd learned to read. I tried to tell him you can't teach children like that, and he said he'd do what he liked with his own children. I said what can an ignorant man like you know about learning — he could hardly read himself. I hit him and knocked him over. His leg was in plaster at the time, because he'd been in an accident at work, and there he sat on the floor, crying, more out of anger than anything but he was humiliated. I was scared, because he could be very violent, so I ran away. I spent two nights sleeping in empty buildings, old houses, you know. It was November, very cold. I got hungry, and I went out and stole some fruit from a market stall. I was very clumsy about it, and somebody saw me and yelled out, and a man ran after me and caught me. I struggled to get away, but there were crowds of people shopping, and they all gathered round in a circle. The thing I remember most about the incident was a woman, a middle-aged woman who said 'Look he's pinched bananas, they always go for things like bananas because they're like monkeys.' Something like that, that was what she meant anyway, and it just broke me up. I started to cry and the man on the stall said was I hungry and I said 'Yes'. A policeman came and took me home. My parents said they would beat me, and that seemed to satisfy him. I was hit about twenty times by my father with the leg of a chair. I've still got scars on my back; it's a wonder it wasn't broken.

I finished up in care, because they split up. I hated

the home I was in. The couple who kept it didn't like children very much, and they spent most of their time behind a door marked Private, while all the kids bashed each other about with toys and broke the windows. I don't know why they called it care, because it wasn't, and they didn't. It was indifference. I don't expect it to be care — all the kids nobody wants, but I don't think they should pretend it is.

Anyway, it did me a good service, because I was allowed to stay on at school. I got O levels, five at one go. I worked in a supermarket at weekends, and holidays; and I stayed on at school and did English and Geography and Religious Knowledge — don't ask me why. I was very Jesus-y for a long time. It never occurred to me that all my problems had anything to do with politics, and I used religion as an escape. Anyway, I got two Bs and a C at A level, and got offered a place at this university without an interview.

The people I worked with in the store were all right to work with, as long as you didn't let it go too far. I went out with a girl called Angie, who was really a bit of a slag, but when her parents knew about it they nearly had the lynch mobs out. She came to me one day and said 'I don't think I ought to see you any more.' I said 'Oh why not'? She said 'It's my parents, they're very upset. My mother thinks it's wrong for people of different colours to marry.' As if I was going to marry her. They all think in these clichés. I suppose I should be grateful that they thought my intentions were honourable, it's a wonder they didn't shout rape, which is the usual reaction.

I've always been an outsider. Not just outside from the white world, that doesn't bother me. But I live in exile from my own home, and in exile from the exiles who live here as well. It used to hurt me a lot; but when I got to university, I began to understand things a bit better. My experience isn't really unique. I've met people who feel about their family and their background just the same as I do. It's a question of class more than race. That's the big issue that gets confused. You try and convince people that they have common interests when all they can see is black and white. I find myself talking with friends sometimes, and I still stop and think, 'Isn't it funny, they're white.' I don't notice it any more most of the time, and the reason is we've got something bigger than colour to unite us. Colour is petty. I'm a Marxist, yes. That gives me my identity, it helps me to understand my historical position. But it doesn't do anything for your personal position. You're still on the outside. Most of the time I try not to think about it.

Barbara McFarlane

*Barbara McFarlane is a secretary in her late forties.
She rents a flat in a house in Liverpool. Her flat is
severely functional, cream-painted wallpaper; an
old-fashioned gas-fire with asbestos nipples glowing
orange; plain yellow upholstered armchairs, with one
or two cigarette burns; a white hearth-rug with
wicker basket and a red cardigan inside in which the
cat sometimes sleeps. A perspex flap has been
contrived in the bottom of the window so that the
cat may come and go as he pleases. In the bookcase
is a large illustrated book called the* Magic of the Cat;
there is a copy of Kenneth Clark's Civilisation *on the
small table, the* North Countrywoman; *by the hearth,
a calendar with a view of Pendle Hill in summer.
Barbara is plump with a pleasant face, greying hair;
she wears a white blouse with a brooch at her throat,
a navy blue cardigan, grey skirt, felt slippers and thick
stockings.*

*We talked of childhood. and its determining
influence on the needs, feelings and responses of
adults.*

My father was a clerk on the railway. He'd been
crippled when he was eighteen, by falling under a
train. At that time of course — he was born in
1887 — there was no possibility of getting artificial
limbs unless you could afford it, and he sat in a chair
at home with his mother who was dying of locomotor
ataxia at that time. There was no compensation, of
course. It was some years before he got artificial
limbs, and then the railway did find him a job as a
clerk. He did quite well really: I never knew how
handicapped he was when I was a child. My mother's
mother had died when she was ten, and as she had
four brothers, she had to be a substitute mother for
the family. The men expected it; and then her father
married, and she had a stepmother, a horrible woman,
a common, coarse sort of woman. So you see, both
my parents had had gaps in their upbringing before
they met each other. They looked for something in
each other that neither could give.

From the beginning I always felt I had no place. My father was simply indifferent, he ignored me completely. But my mother tortured me. My childhood was a time of misery. She wouldn't leave me alone. She forced me to be self-sufficient, and then refused to let me get on with it. I could never do a thing right. Try as I might, I could not please her. If I did something it was wrong; and if I did the opposite that was wrong too. If I heard her say 'Oh I like so-and-so', I'd save up until I could buy her whatever it was, and she'd say 'Oh I don't like that'. I remember I once drew a picture for her — of a horse, I loved horses, the Shire horses that had to pull the trams up the steep slopes of the town, and I took it to her and she said something disparaging. I tore it into little pieces.

I felt I was an intrusion into their lives. I was always awkward and clumsy as a child. My sister was prettier, more feminine. I was an interloper, there was no place for me. Some distant relatives of my mother — people she didn't even know — left her a small draper's shop. That was what she really wanted to be, a businesswoman. I remember the sign over the shop 'Fancy Draper'. When I was born she had to close the shop down for a long time because she was very ill. She'd been told not to have any more children, and so there was another cause for resentment. I can see that she was an intelligent woman, and she really wanted something more than being simply a housewife. I can understand them both now, I certainly don't feel any resentment now. I've learned to accept and to love them.

Outside the house of course I used to run wild. I had lots of mates — boys, and to all intents and purposes I was one of them. I remember one day I had an uncle called Uncle Charley, and I think they expected him to leave them some money or something, we always had to be on our best behaviour with him. I'd been dressed up in my best dress to wait for him to arrive. I went out, and somehow I got into a boxing match with some of the lads, real gloves on, it was marvellous, I got my nose all bloody, and I stained the front of my dress with the blood, I was such a mess. I knew there'd be hell to pay, but I couldn't help it. It was me, I'd alway had, ever since I could remember, more of the male in me than female. I've been aware of having a male mentality and attitudes in a female body.

My parents were very sad really. They had no way of expressing emotion. I was in the WRAF later, and I'd really begun to get free of them and make my own life by then; and I came home on leave, and my father sat there, feeling very sorry for himself, complaining of earache. I got some warm olive oil and put it into his ear and plugged it with cotton wool. At first he said 'Don't fuss', but after a while it felt better and he said 'Eh, that's better', and I looked at him and there were tears running down his face. And he went round telling everybody what I'd done for him. I'd only put olive oil in his ear for God's sake. But it meant so much more. He was so undemonstrative, everything had had to be choked back.

When I was adolescent, I fell in love for the first time. As my companions had always been boys, I fell in love with a girl. I'd always despised girls, shoved them out of the way; so when it happened, I was shattered in one way, but found it perfectly natural in another. And then one day, I was out with some of my boy-friends, and I heard one of them talking about all the things he'd done or was going to do with this girl, my girl. My first reaction was to fight, but then I realised — I had no right to set myself up as his rival. So I was made lonely, first of all by my natural inheritance, and then by my parents' rejection of me, and then by the dawning discovery that I had a man's psyche in female form.

But don't think my life has been all misery. Far from it. I've known a great deal of joy, and happiness. Even at the time of my greatest suffering there were so many consolations; and even then, the misery contained the seeds of my own reconciliation to it. I'd always gone out into the countryside, Pendle Hill, the Ribble Valley. Look, there's Pendle Hill on the calendar. I used to draw, walk, lie in the long grass watching the life of the insects in the grass, and I used to think 'Perhaps God is like that, looking down on us just as I'm looking at the life swarming in the grass'. I'd always loved animals, not in a sentimental way, not as pets, but with respect for their independence and autonomous life. I'd felt the strength of life in running water and trees, just as I did in the lovely Shire horses and cats. In the past few years I've come to see that everything in nature is connected, is inter-dependent; it's such a beautiful structure, everything tends towards harmony, completeness, wholeness. I've come to see that everything has meaning in the whole. The inanimate things I had to turn to as a child were part of a greater pattern — just as I must be, with all my awkwardness and clumsiness.

I feel free now, I feel happier than I ever did. I've come to see something of God's scheme of things, and to accept my place in it. I feel free of all the turbulence, of not understanding myself, of trying to conform to something I'm not, of giving way to self-pity. Believe me, now that I'm nearly fifty, I'm free of any desire to belong to the world of ordinary, normal people. I feel I'm making a fresh start, in the life of the spirit. Everything seems to make sense at last. My loneliness *is* me. I'm no longer lonely because I've ceased to look for human kinship at the deep level I used to long for. I would so dearly have loved to *share*, I once thought it might be possible, but now I know it isn't.

Afterword

Loneliness is a vague term. Many people believe that they have a right to be happy. When they are not, they feel bitter and cheated. Others inhabit misery and despair as their natural element. There are no criteria to assess the prevalence or intensity of the loneliness people admit to. It is often used as a synonym for lack of fulfilment, unhappiness or failure in many areas of experience. All that I have been able to do in this book is to indicate, tentatively, some of the areas of social isolation which recur in people's accounts of themselves.